HARCOURT

SOCIAL Studies

A Child's View

HOUGHTON MIFFLIN HARCOURT
School Publishers

HARCOURT SOCIAL Studies

A Child's View

Series Authors

Dr. Michael J. Berson
Professor
Social Science Education
University of South Florida
Tampa, Florida

Dr. Tyrone C. Howard
Associate Professor
UCLA Graduate School of Education & Information Studies
University of California at Los Angeles
Los Angeles, California

Dr. Cinthia Salinas
Assistant Professor
Department of Curriculum and Instruction
College of Education
The University of Texas at Austin
Austin, Texas

Series Consultants

Dr. Marsha Alibrandi
Assistant Professor
Social Studies Teacher Education
Department of Curriculum and Instruction
Graduate School of Education and Allied Professions
Fairfield University
Fairfield, Connecticut

Dr. Patricia G. Avery
Professor
College of Education and Human Development
University of Minnesota
Minneapolis/St. Paul, Minnesota

Dr. Linda Bennett
Associate Professor
College of Education
University of Missouri–Columbia
Columbia, Missouri

Dr. Walter C. Fleming
Department Head and Professor
Native American Studies
Montana State University
Bozeman, Montana

Dr. S. G. Grant
Dean
School of Education
Binghamton University
Binghamton, New York

C. C. Herbison
Lecturer
African and African-American Studies
University of Kansas
Lawrence, Kansas

Dr. Eric Johnson
Assistant Professor
Director, Urban Education Program
School of Education
Drake University
Des Moines, Iowa

Dr. Bruce E. Larson
Professor
Social Studies Education
Secondary Education
Woodring College of Education
Western Washington University
Bellingham, Washington

Dr. Merry M. Merryfield
Professor
Social Studies and Global Education
College of Education
The Ohio State University
Columbus, Ohio

Dr. Peter Rees
Associate Professor
Department of Geography
University of Delaware
Wilmington, Delaware

Dr. Phillip J. VanFossen
James F. Ackerman Professor of Social Studies Education
Director, James F. Ackerman Center for Democratic Citizenship
Associate Director, Purdue Center for Economic Education
Purdue University
West Lafayette, Indiana

Dr. Myra Zarnowski
Professor
Elementary and Early Childhood Education
Queens College
The City University of New York
Flushing, New York

Classroom Reviewers and Contributors

Alicia Campbell
Teacher
Oakmont Elementary School
Columbus, Ohio

Jennifer Cook
Teacher
Walton-Verona Elementary School
Verona, Kentucky

Shirley Garlington
Teacher
Amboy Elementary School
North Little Rock, Arkansas

Amy Gibson
Teacher
Winds West Elementary School
Oklahoma City, Oklahoma

Vicki Kinder
Teacher
Oak Elementary School
Bartlett, Tennessee

Martha K. Lennon
Teacher
Virginia Lake School
Palatine, Illinois

Kathy Price
Teacher
Rivercrest Elementary School
Bartlett, Tennessee

11   Introduction: Time, People, Place

14   Reading Your Textbook

18   Geography Review

Unit 1

Rules and Laws

2   Unit 1 Preview Vocabulary

4   Focus Skill **Reading Social Studies:
     Cause and Effect**

6   **Start with a Poem
     "Friendship's Rule"**
     by M. Lucille Ford
     illustrated by Stacy Peterson

10   **Lesson 1 School Rules**

14   **Critical Thinking Skills**
     Solve a Problem

16   **Lesson 2 Community Rules**

20   **Map and Globe Skills**
     Read a Map

22   **Lesson 3 People Lead the Way**

26   **Citizenship Skills**
     Make a Choice by Voting

28   **Lesson 4 Government Helps Us**

32   **Citizenship**
      Police Officers and You

34   **Lesson 5 Our Rights**

38   **Citizenship Skills**
      Work and Play Together

40   **Biography**
      Rosa Parks

42   **Fun with Social Studies**

44   Unit I Review and
      Test Prep

48   Unit I Activities

Unit 2

Where People Live

50   Unit 2 Preview Vocabulary

52   **Reading Social Studies:** **Categorize and Classify** (Focus Skill)

54   **Start with a Poem** **"Making Maps"** by Elaine V. Emans illustrated by Rob Dunlavey

56   **Lesson 1 Finding Where You Are**

60   **Map and Globe Skills** Use a Globe

62   **Lesson 2 Land and Water**

66   **Field Trip** Great Smoky Mountains National Park

68   **Lesson 3 People and Places**

72   **Map and Globe Skills**
Find Directions on a Map

74   **Lesson 4 People Use Resources**

80   **Study Skills**
Build Vocabulary

82   **Biography**
George Washington Carver

84   **Lesson 5 What's the Weather?**

88   **Points of View**

90   **Fun with Social Studies**

92   Unit 2 Review and Test Prep

96   Unit 2 Activities

Unit 3

We Love Our Country

98   Unit 3 Preview Vocabulary

100   **Reading Social Studies: Main Idea and Details**

102   **Start with a Song "America"**
by Samuel F. Smith
illustrated by Richard Johnson

104   **Lesson 1 Our Country Begins**

110   **Biography**
George Washington

112   **Primary Sources**
Learning About Freedom

116   **Lesson 2 I Pledge Allegiance**

120 **Lesson 3 American Symbols**

124 **Chart and Graph Skills**
Read a Diagram

126 **Field Trip**
The Liberty Bell

128 **Lesson 4 Holidays and Heroes**

134 **Chart and Graph Skills**
Read a Calendar

136 **Citizenship**
Flag Day

138 **Fun with Social Studies**

140 Unit 3 Review and Test Prep

144 Unit 3 Activities

Unit 4

Our Changing World

146   Unit 4 Preview Vocabulary

148   **Focus Skill** **Reading Social Studies: Sequence**

150   **Start with a Story**
Aunt Flossie's Hats
by Elizabeth Fitzgerald Howard
paintings by James Ransome

158   **Lesson 1 People Long Ago**

164   **Study Skills**
Use Visuals

166   **Primary Sources**
Home Tools

170   **Lesson 2 Schools Long Ago**

176   **Chart and Graph Skills**
Put Things in Groups

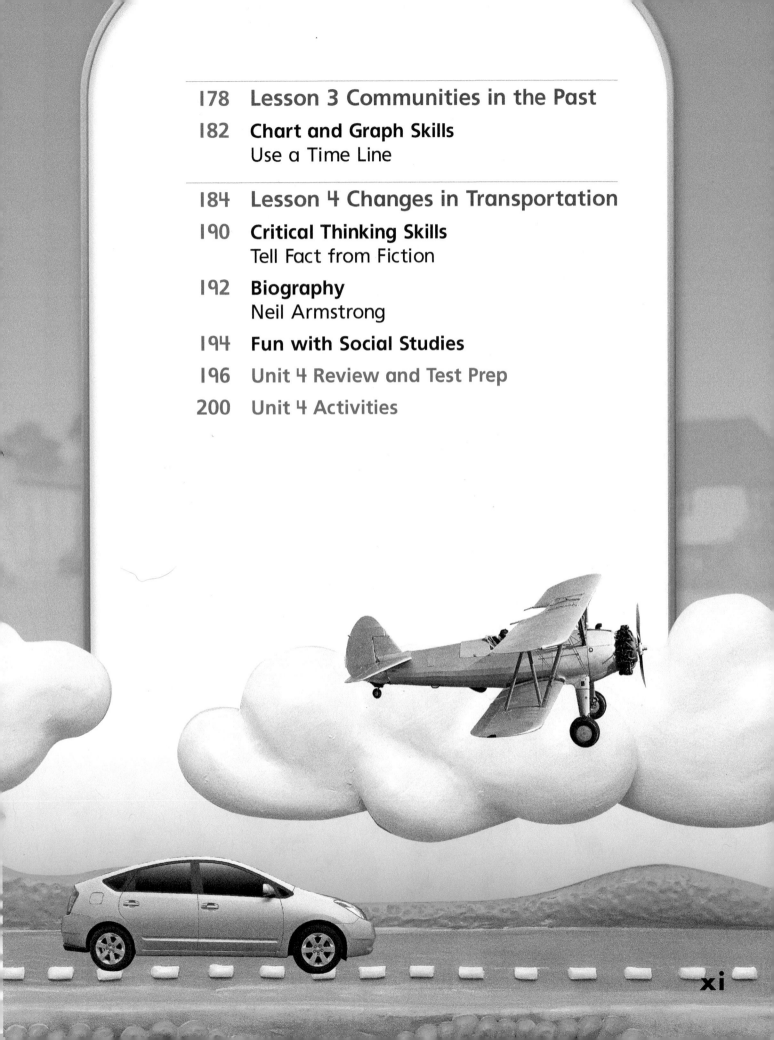

178 **Lesson 3 Communities in the Past**

182 **Chart and Graph Skills**
Use a Time Line

184 **Lesson 4 Changes in Transportation**

190 **Critical Thinking Skills**
Tell Fact from Fiction

192 **Biography**
Neil Armstrong

194 **Fun with Social Studies**

196 Unit 4 Review and Test Prep

200 Unit 4 Activities

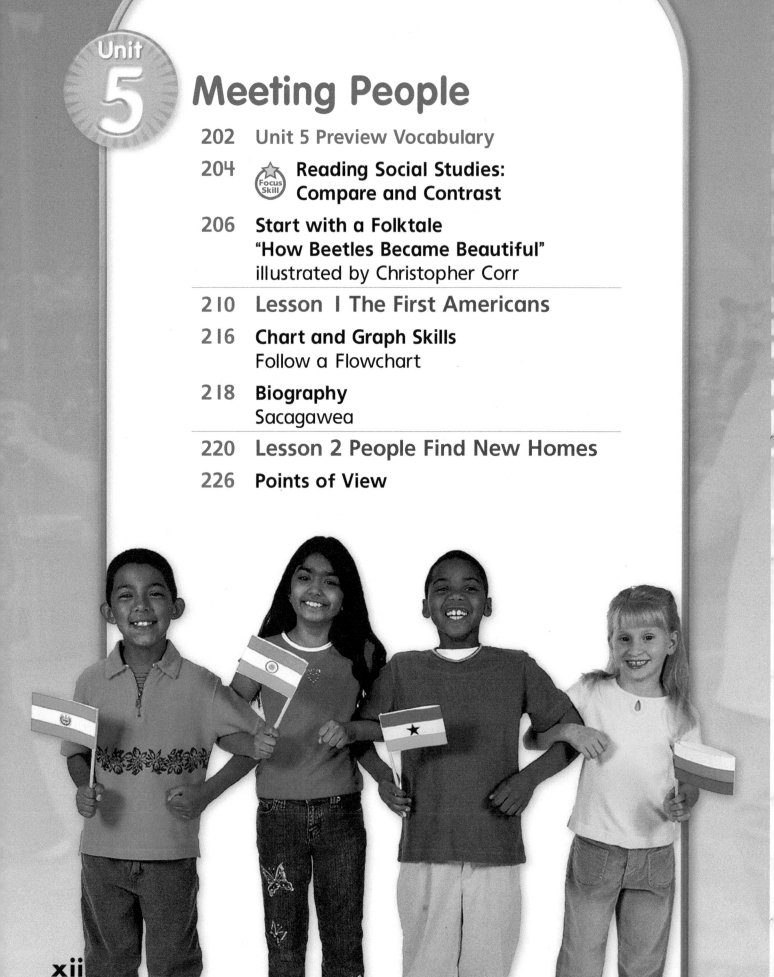

Unit 5

Meeting People

202   Unit 5 Preview Vocabulary

204   Focus Skill   **Reading Social Studies: Compare and Contrast**

206   **Start with a Folktale** **"How Beetles Became Beautiful"** illustrated by Christopher Corr

210   **Lesson 1 The First Americans**

216   **Chart and Graph Skills** Follow a Flowchart

218   **Biography** Sacagawea

220   **Lesson 2 People Find New Homes**

226   **Points of View**

228 **Lesson 3 Expressing Culture**

232 **Lesson 4 Sharing Celebrations**

236 **Map and Globe Skills**
Follow a Route

238 **Lesson 5 Families Around the World**

242 **Fun with Social Studies**

244 Unit 5 Review and Test Prep

248 Unit 5 Activities

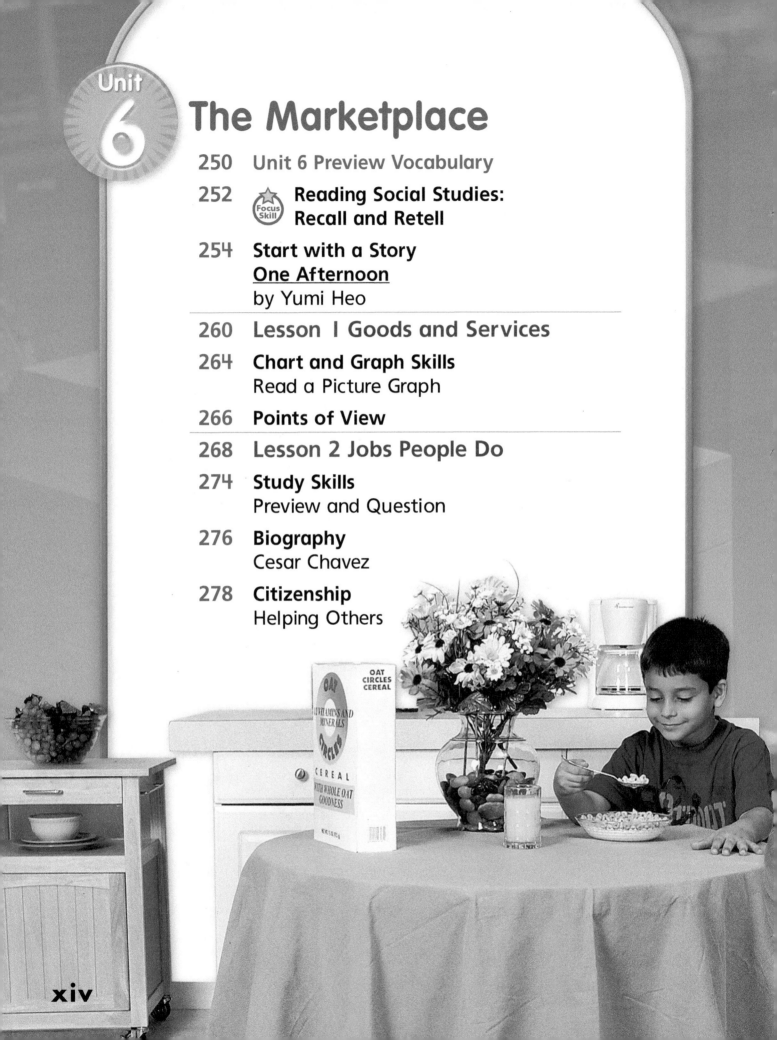

Unit 6

The Marketplace

250   Unit 6 Preview Vocabulary

252   Reading Social Studies:
      Recall and Retell

254   Start with a Story
      One Afternoon
      by Yumi Heo

260   Lesson 1 Goods and Services

264   Chart and Graph Skills
      Read a Picture Graph

266   Points of View

268   Lesson 2 Jobs People Do

274   Study Skills
      Preview and Question

276   Biography
      Cesar Chavez

278   Citizenship
      Helping Others

280 **Lesson 3 Buyers and Sellers**

286 **Critical Thinking Skills**
Make a Choice When Buying

288 **Field Trip**
Royal Oak Farmers Market

290 **Lesson 4 Working in a Factory**

296 **Chart and Graph Skills**
Use a Bar Graph

298 **Fun with Social Studies**

300 Unit 6 Review and Test Prep

304 Unit 6 Activities

FOR YOUR REFERENCE

R2 Atlas

R10 Research Handbook

R18 Biographical Dictionary

R20 Picture Glossary

R37 Index

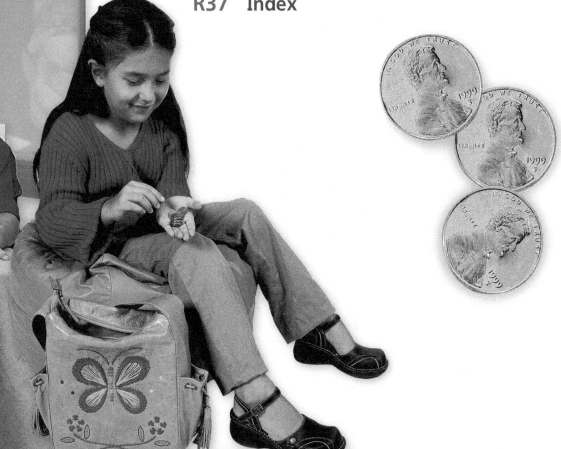

Features

Skills

Chart and Graph Skills

124 Read a Diagram
134 Read a Calendar
176 Put Things in Groups
182 Use a Time Line
216 Follow a Flowchart
264 Read a Picture Graph
296 Use a Bar Graph

Citizenship Skills

26 Make a Choice by Voting
38 Work and Play Together

Critical Thinking Skills

14 Solve a Problem
190 Tell Fact from Fiction
286 Make a Choice When Buying

Map and Globe Skills

20 Read a Map
60 Use a Globe
72 Find Directions on a Map
236 Follow a Route

Reading Social Studies

4 Cause and Effect
52 Categorize and Classify
100 Main Idea and Details
148 Sequence
204 Compare and Contrast
252 Recall and Retell

Study Skills

80 Build Vocabulary
164 Use Visuals
274 Preview and Question

Citizenship

32 Police Officers and You
136 Flag Day
278 Helping Others

Points of View

88 Where You Live
226 Cultures in Your Community
266 Important Goods and Services

Literature and Music

6 "Friendship's Rule"
by M. Lucille Ford
illustrated by Stacy Peterson

54 "Making Maps"
by Elaine V. Emans
illustrated by Rob Dunlavey

102 "America"
by Samuel F. Smith
illustrated by Richard Johnson

150 Aunt Flossie's Hats
by Elizabeth Fitzgerald Howard
paintings by James Ransome

206 "How Beetles Became Beautiful"
illustrated by Christopher Corr

254 One Afternoon
by Yumi Heo

Primary Sources

112 Learning About Freedom
166 Home Tools

Documents

112 Page from John Adams's Journal
114 The Declaration of Independence
115 The United States Constitution

Biography

40 Rosa Parks
82 George Washington Carver
110 George Washington
192 Neil Armstrong
218 Sacagawea
276 Cesar Chavez

Children in History

70 Laura Ingalls Wilder
174 George S. Parker
271 Addie Laird

Field Trip

66 Great Smoky Mountains National Park
126 The Liberty Bell
288 Royal Oak Farmers Market

Fun with Social Studies

42 Fun Town Walk
90 Life on the Farm
138 They're Hiding
194 Find the Changes
242 How Coyote Got Thin
298 You're in Business!

Charts, Graphs, and Diagrams

5 Cause and Effect
26 Ballot
27 Vote Tally Chart
47 Votes for a Class Pet
53 Categorize and Classify
80 Word Web
101 Main Idea and Details
125 The Statue of Liberty
135 February Calendar
142 January Calendar
143 United States Capitol
149 Sequence
177 School Tools
198 Transportation
205 Compare and Contrast
217 How the Chumash Indians Made Acorn Soup
246 How to Make a Chinese Lantern
253 Recall and Retell
265 Baskets of Apples Sold
275 K-W-L Chart
283 How Money Moves
297 Boxes of Crayons Sold
302 Mr. Wilson's Toy Store
303 Mr. Wheel's Car Repair Service

Maps

21 Appleton
24 Kentucky
46 Where I Live
56 Community Map
57 Cities in Indiana
58 United States
59 Oklahoma
61 Western Hemisphere
61 Eastern Hemisphere
73 Greenville
95 The Zoo
106 The 13 Colonies
113 The 13 Colonies, 1775
214 Native American Crafts
237 Parade Route
247 Bus Route
I11 Home Address
R2 World Continents
R4 World Land and Water
R6 United States States and Capitals
R8 United States Land and Water

Time Lines

41 Rosa Parks Time Line
83 George Washington Carver Time Line
111 George Washington Time Line
182 Marc's Time Line
193 Neil Armstrong Time Line
199 Mary's Time Line
219 Sacagawea Time Line
277 Cesar Chavez Time Line

The Story Well Told

"America! America!
God shed his grace on thee
And crown thy good with brotherhood
From sea to shining sea!"

"America the Beautiful" by Katharine Lee Bates

Do you ever wonder about your world? This year you will be learning how our country has grown over **time**. You will read about the **people** in your world and how they get along. Also, you will compare the ways people live in many different **places**.

A Child's View

You can learn more about yourself by looking at people who lived before you.

Americans share many ideas.

Your view of the world may depend on where you live.

Reading Your Textbook

GETTING STARTED

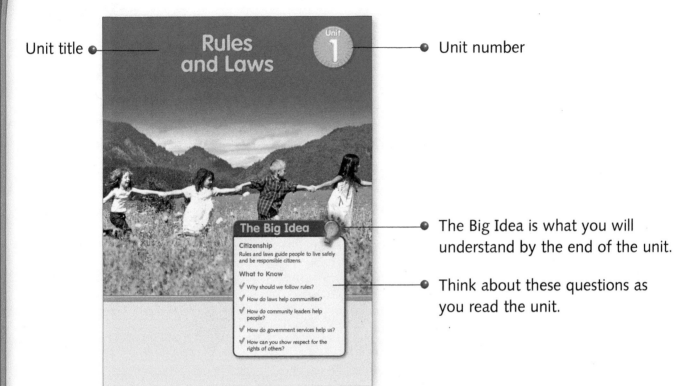

Unit title

Unit number

The Big Idea is what you will understand by the end of the unit.

Think about these questions as you read the unit.

PREVIEW VOCABULARY

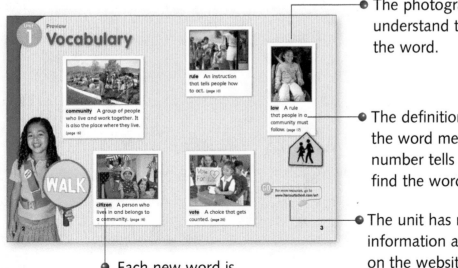

The photograph helps you understand the meaning of the word.

The definition tells you what the word means. The page number tells you where to find the word in this unit.

The unit has more information and activities on the website.

Each new word is highlighted in yellow.

READING SOCIAL STUDIES

Reading skill and explanation

Model paragraph for reading practice

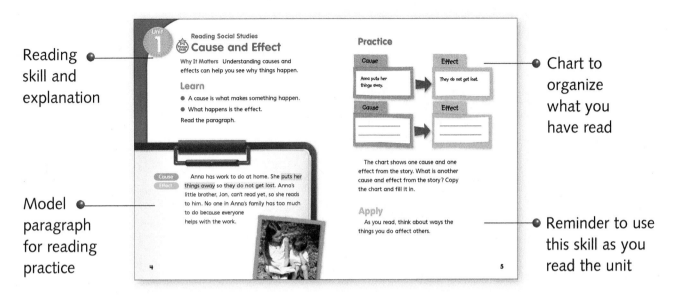

Chart to organize what you have read

Reminder to use this skill as you read the unit

START WITH LITERATURE

Every unit starts with a story, play, poem, song, article, or folktale.

Questions to practice the unit reading skill and to talk about personal experiences

READING A LESSON

Lesson number

Guiding question

New words to learn

Reminder to use your reading skill

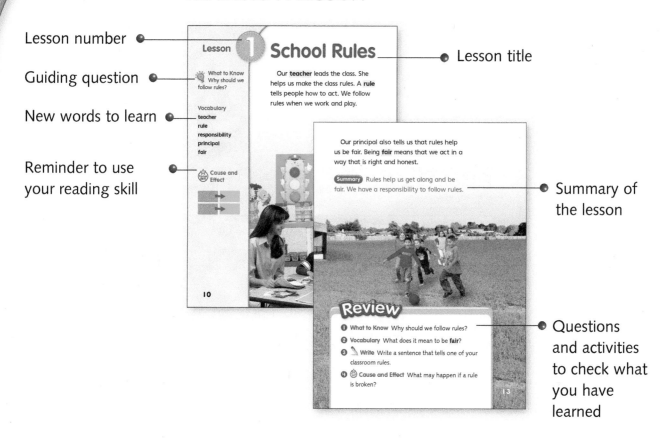

Lesson title

Summary of the lesson

Questions and activities to check what you have learned

PRACTICING SKILLS

Skill lessons help you build your map and globe, chart and graph, study, critical thinking, and citizenship skills.

Skill category

Skill lesson title

Why the skill is important

Steps to learn the skill

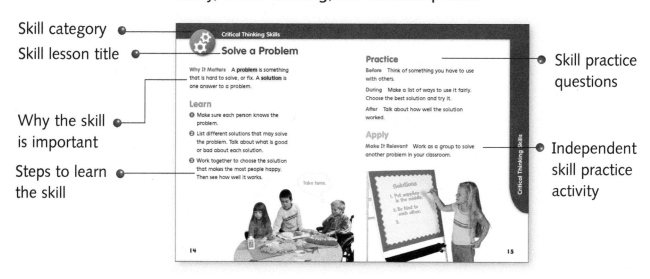

Skill practice questions

Independent skill practice activity

SPECIAL FEATURES

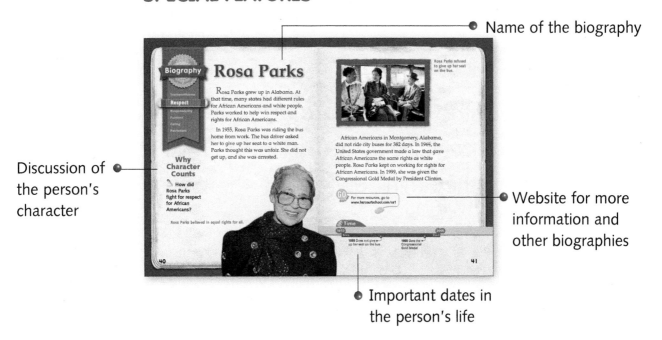

Name of the biography

Discussion of the person's character

Website for more information and other biographies

Important dates in the person's life

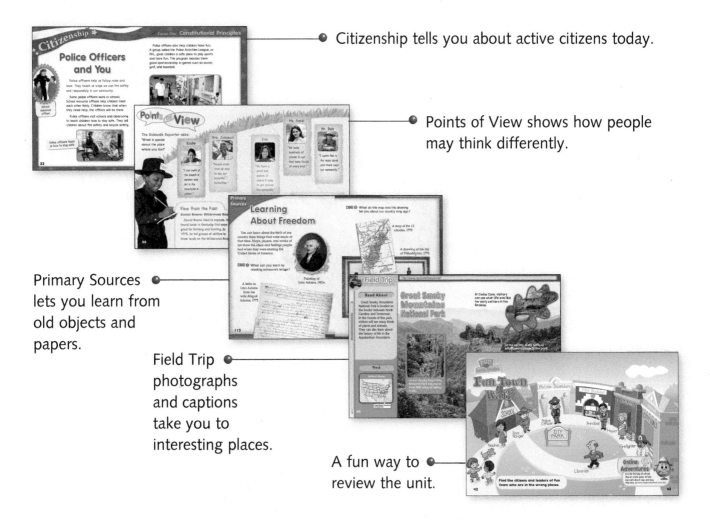

Citizenship tells you about active citizens today.

Points of View shows how people may think differently.

Primary Sources lets you learn from old objects and papers.

Field Trip photographs and captions take you to interesting places.

A fun way to review the unit.

Go to the Reference section in the back of this book to see other special features.

The Five Themes of Geography

The story of people is also the story of where they live. When scientists talk about Earth, they think about five themes or main ideas.

Location

Everything on Earth has its own place.

Place

Every place has features that make it different from other places.

GEOGRAPHY

Human-Environment Interactions

People can change their surroundings.

Movement

Each day, people around the world trade goods and ideas.

THEMES

Regions

Areas of Earth share features that make them different from other areas.

Where Do You Live?

Families have addresses. An **address** tells where people live. It has a number and a street name. Read Sam's address.

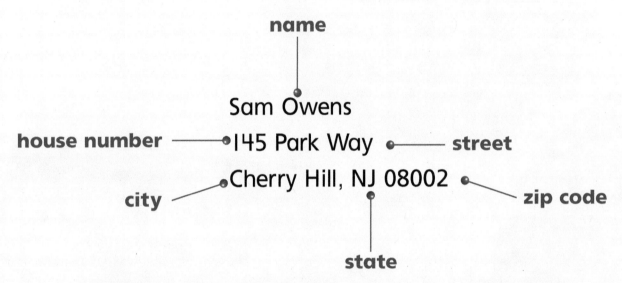

name

Sam Owens

house number —— 145 Park Way •—— street

city —— Cherry Hill, NJ 08002 •—— zip code

state

PARK WAY

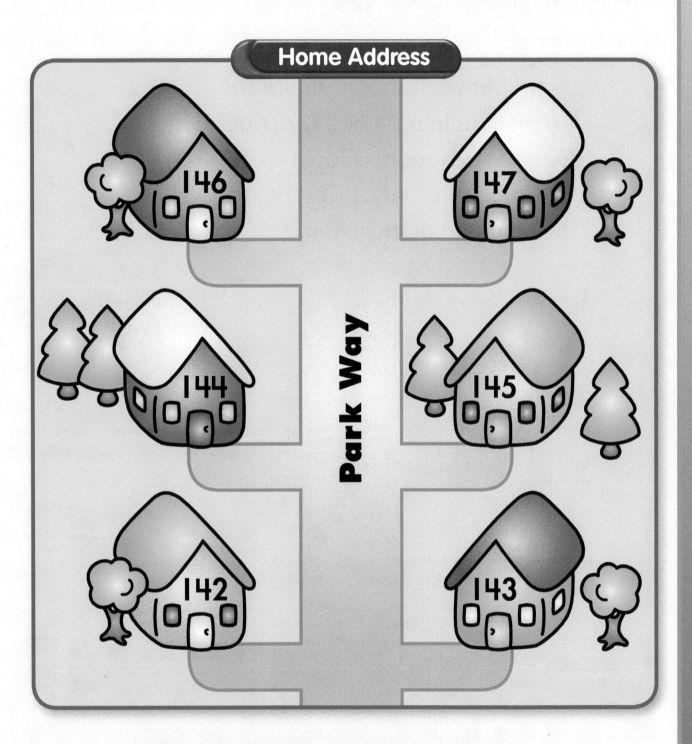

Look at the map. Find Sam's house.

What is the number of his neighbor's

house across the street?

Where Are You?

Look at the drawing of a school from above. It shows where the rooms are in a school. Describe where each room is located. Use words such as **left**, **right**, **next to**, **beside**, and **across from**.

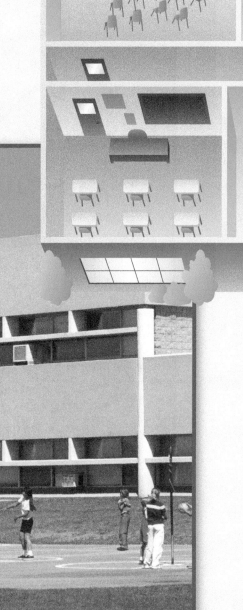

MIDDLETON HEIGHTS ELEMENTARY

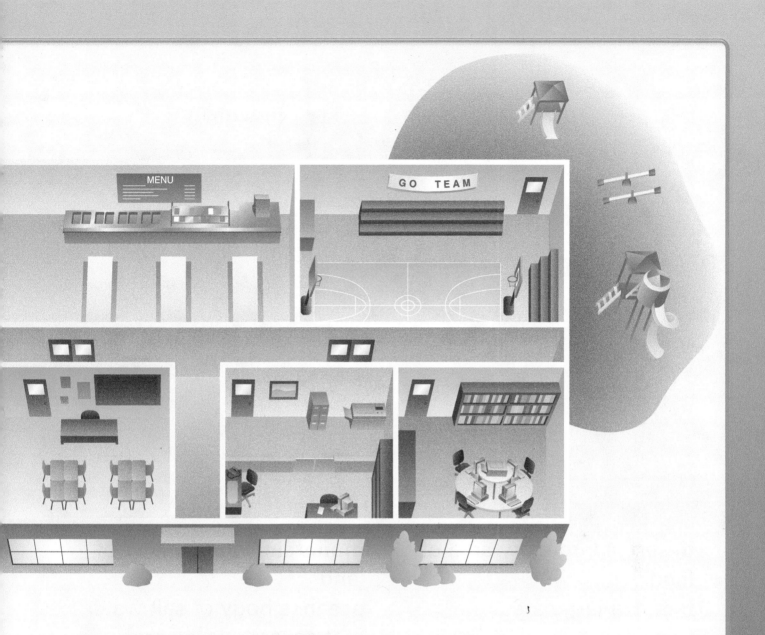

1 How is this school like your school?

2 Imagine you are helping a child who is new to your school. Describe how to get to the rooms he or she might need to find.

mountain

valley

river

plain

desert

forest

hill

lake

peninsula

gulf

island

ocean

desert a large, dry area of land

forest a large area of trees

gulf a large body of ocean water that is partly surrounded by land

hill land that rises above the land around it

island a landform with water all around it

lake a body of water with land on all sides

mountain highest kind of land

ocean a body of salt water that covers a large area

peninsula a landform that is surrounded on only three sides by water

plain flat land

river a large stream of water that flows across the land

valley low land between hills or mountains

Rules and Laws

The Big Idea

Citizenship
Rules and laws guide people to live safely and be responsible citizens.

What to Know

✔ Why should we follow rules?

✔ How do laws help communities?

✔ How do community leaders help people?

✔ How do government services help us?

✔ How can you show respect for the rights of others?

Rules and Laws

Citizenship

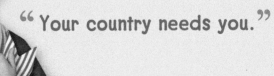

"Your country needs you."

"Everyone should vote."

"Respect people's rights."

Vocabulary

community A group of people who live and work together. It is also the place where they live.

(page 16)

citizen A person who lives in and belongs to a community. (page 16)

rule An instruction that tells people how to act. (page 10)

law A rule that people in a community must follow. (page 17)

vote A choice that gets counted. (page 26)

GO ONLINE For more resources, go to www.harcourtschool.com/ss1

3

Reading Social Studies

 Focus Skill

Cause and Effect

Why It Matters Understanding causes and effects can help you see why things happen.

Learn

- A cause is what makes something happen.
- What happens is the effect.

Read the paragraph.

Cause
Effect

Anna has work to do at home. She puts her things away so they do not get lost. Anna's little brother, Jon, can't read yet, so she reads to him. No one in Anna's family has too much to do because everyone helps with the work.

Practice

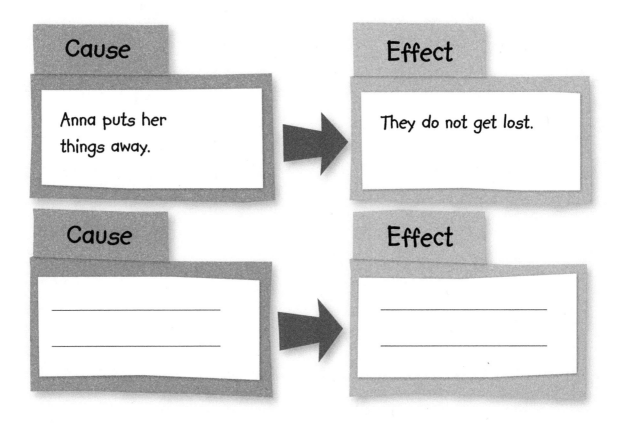

Cause		Effect
Anna puts her things away.	→	They do not get lost.

Cause		Effect
_____ _____	→	_____ _____

The chart shows one cause and one effect from the story. What is another cause and effect from the story? Copy the chart and fill it in.

Apply

As you read, think about ways the things you do affect others.

Friendship's Rule

by M. Lucille Ford

illustrated by Stacy Peterson

Our teacher says there is a rule
We should remember while at school,

At home, at play, whate'er we do,
And that's the rule of friendship true.

7

If you would have friends, you must do
To them the kindly things that you

Would like to have them do and say
To you while at your work and play.

And that's the rule of friendship true;
It works in all we say and do.

It pays to be a friend polite,
For friendship's rule is always right.

Response Corner

① (Focus Skill) **Cause and Effect**   What could happen if you do not follow friendship's rule?

② **Make It Relevant**   Draw a picture of you and a friend following friendship's rule.

School Rules

Vocabulary

teacher

rule

responsibility

principal

fair

 **Cause and Effect**

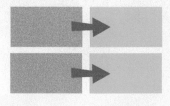

Our **teacher** leads the class. She helps us make the class rules. A **rule** tells people how to act. We follow rules when we work and play.

At school, rules help us learn and get along. Rules also help us stay safe. This is why we have a responsibility to follow rules. A **responsibility** is something you should do.

Be kind.

Follow directions.

Take turns.

Work quietly.

Our **principal** leads the whole school. He tells us that different parts of the school have different rules. We walk quietly in the hall. When we play outside, we do not have to be quiet.

Our principal also tells us that rules help us be fair. Being **fair** means that we act in a way that is right and honest.

Summary Rules help us get along and be fair. We have a responsibility to follow rules.

Review

1. **What to Know** Why should we follow rules?

2. **Vocabulary** What does it mean to be **fair**?

3. ✏️ **Write** Write a sentence that tells one of your classroom rules.

4. 🌟 (Focus Skill) **Cause and Effect** What may happen if a rule is broken?

Solve a Problem

Why It Matters   A **problem** is something that is hard to solve, or fix. A **solution** is one answer to a problem.

Learn

1 Make sure each person knows the problem.

2 List different solutions that may solve the problem. Talk about what is good or bad about each solution.

3 Work together to choose the solution that makes the most people happy. Then see how well it works.

Take turns.

14

Practice

Before   Think of something you have to use with others.

During   Make a list of ways to use it fairly. Choose the best solution and try it.

After   Talk about how well the solution worked.

Apply

Make It Relevant   Work as a group to solve another problem in your classroom.

Solutions
1. Put supplies in the middle.
2. Be kind to each other.
3.

What to Know
How do laws
help communities?

Vocabulary
community
citizen
law

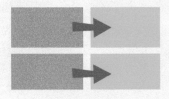

**Cause and
Effect**

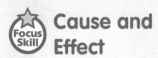

Community Rules

This is my community.
A **community** is a place where
people live and work together.
A person who lives in and belongs
to a community is a **citizen**.

16

Communities have rules called laws. A **law** is a rule that people in a community must follow. Communities can have many kinds of laws.

Jonesborough, Tennessee

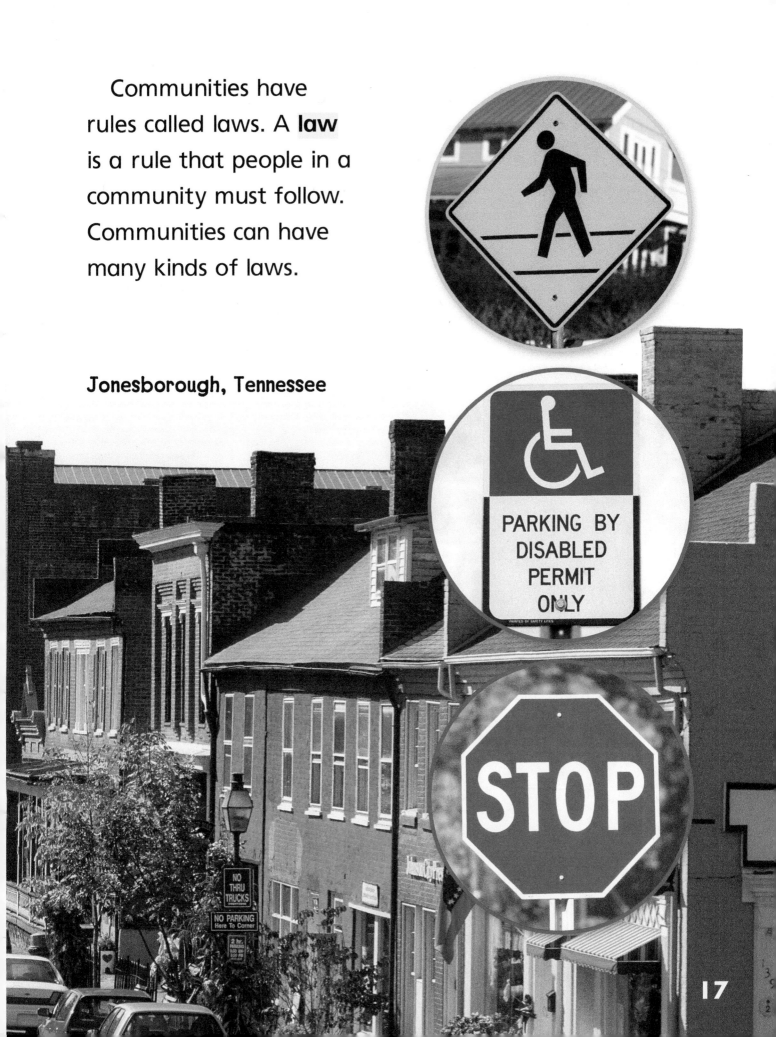

Laws are important for citizens in a community. They tell people how to live together safely. They also help keep communities clean.

Sometimes people do not follow laws. Breaking laws causes problems. People who cross the street at the wrong place may get hurt.

Summary Laws help people live together safely in a community.

Review

1. **What to Know** How do laws help communities?

2. **Vocabulary** What is a **citizen**?

3. **Activity** Draw a picture that shows you and your family following a law in your community.

4. **Cause and Effect** What can happen if you do not follow a law?

19

Read a Map

Why It Matters   A **map** is a picture that shows where places are. You can use symbols to help you read a map. A **symbol** is a picture or an object that stands for something.

Learn

Maps use symbols to show places. A **map key** shows you what each symbol on the map stands for.

Practice

1 What places do you see on the map?

2 What symbol shows the fire station?

3 Where would you go to buy food?

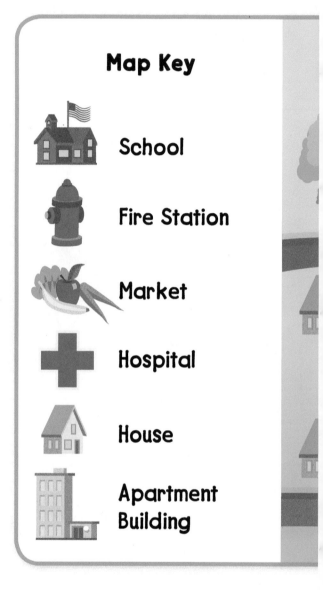

Map Key

School

Fire Station

Market

Hospital

House

Apartment Building

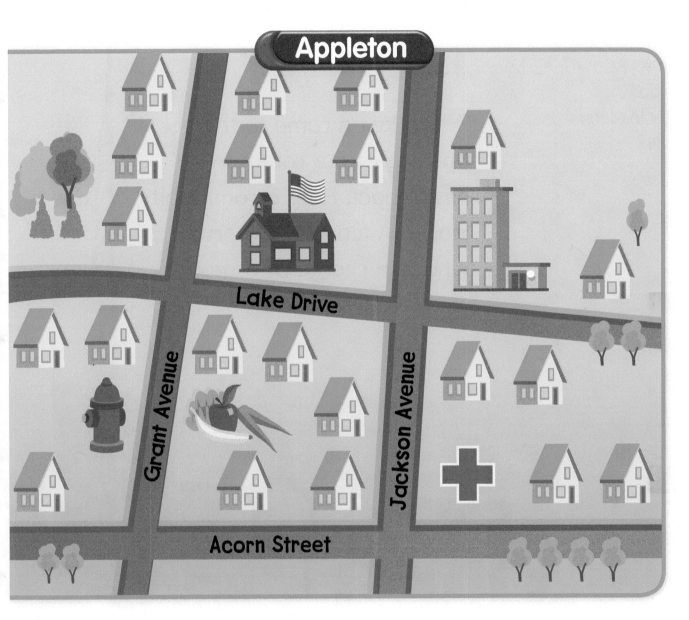

Appleton

Lake Drive

Grant Avenue

Jackson Avenue

Acorn Street

Apply

Make It Relevant Make a map of your school.
Use symbols and a map key to show places.

For online activities, go to
www.harcourtschool.com/ss1

People Lead the Way

What to Know
How do community leaders help people?

Vocabulary

leader

mayor

city

government

governor

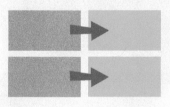

Cause and Effect

Yim Kwan came to the opening of our community's new school. He is a community leader. A **leader** is a person who is in charge of a group.

22

Leaders help groups make and follow rules. They also help groups solve problems.

Yim Kwan is our mayor. A **mayor** is the leader of a city. A **city** is a large community.

Mayor Kwan

Mayor Kwan helps open our new school.

People in a community choose the leaders they want for their government. A **government** is a group of people who lead a community. Mayor Kwan leads the city government.

States also have their own governments. A **governor** leads the state government.

Capitol building

There are many kinds of leaders in our community. My mom is a softball coach, so she is a leader. Teachers, club leaders, and ministers are also leaders.

Summary Leaders help people follow rules and solve problems in the community.

Review

① **What to Know** How do community leaders help people?

② **Vocabulary** What does a **mayor** do?

③ **Activity** Draw a picture that shows a leader helping people in your community.

④ **Focus Skill** **Cause and Effect** Think about a time when a leader helped you solve a problem. What did he or she do?

Make a Choice by Voting

Why It Matters   When you **vote**, you make a choice that gets counted. Americans vote for many government leaders, such as the President. The **President** is the leader of our country. Americans also vote to make choices about laws.

Learn

You can use a ballot to vote. A **ballot** shows all the choices. You mark your choice on it. The choice that gets the most votes wins.

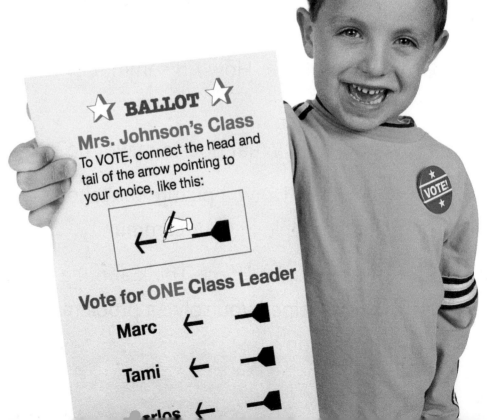

★ BALLOT ★
Mrs. Johnson's Class
To VOTE, connect the head and tail of the arrow pointing to your choice, like this:

Vote for ONE Class Leader

Marc

Tami

Practice

① Mrs. Johnson's class used ballots to vote for a class leader. The choices were Marc, Tami, and Carlos.

② Look at the chart. Count all the votes to see who will be the class leader.

Apply

Make It Relevant List some games your class would like to play. Make ballots, and have each person vote. Count the votes and show them on a chart. Which game got the most votes?

 What to Know
How do government services help us?

Vocabulary
government service

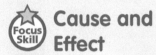
 Cause and Effect (Focus Skill)

Government Helps Us

Government services are things that a government does to make a community a good place to live in. Government workers keep communities safe and clean.

Police officers keep us safe by making sure that people follow the laws. Firefighters help when there is a fire.

Park rangers make sure parks stay clean. They also help park visitors stay safe. Government workers build roads and highways in the community.

Schools and libraries are also government services. Teachers help us learn. Librarians help us find books to read.

Summary Government services help keep our communities safe and clean.

Review

1. **What to Know** How do government services help us?

2. **Vocabulary** What is one **government service** in your community?

3. **Activity** Draw a picture of a government worker doing his or her job.

4. **Cause and Effect** What would happen if there were no police officers or firefighters?

Police Officers and You

Police officers help us follow rules and laws. They teach us ways we can live safely and responsibly in our community.

Some police officers work in schools. School resource officers help children treat each other fairly. Children know that when they need help, the officers will be there.

Police officers visit schools and classrooms to teach children how to stay safe. They tell children about fire safety and bicycle safety.

School resource officer

Police officers teach us how to stay safe.

Police officers also help children have fun. A group called the Police Activities League, or PAL, gives children a safe place to play sports and have fun. The program teaches them good sportsmanship in games such as soccer, golf, and baseball.

Police officers help us have fun, too.

Make It Relevant How do police officers help people in your community?

Our Rights

💡 **What to Know**
How can you show respect for the rights of others?

Vocabulary

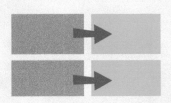

⭐ **Focus Skill** **Cause and Effect**

To show **respect** is to treat someone or something well. I show respect for my teacher by listening to him and following rules.

We can also show respect for others by being responsible in the way we act. One way to be responsible is to help others.

Fast Fact!

A wise man in China named Confucius taught the Golden Rule more than 2,500 years ago. The Golden Rule says to treat others the way you want to be treated.

35

Americans have rights.
A **right** is something people
are free to do. They are free
to speak about their ideas.
They can belong to groups.
They are free to worship
where they choose.

Free to worship

Free to speak

When people have rights, they also have responsibilities. One responsibility is to follow rules. By following rules and laws, we show respect for other people's rights.

Summary We can show respect for others by being responsible.

Review

① **What to Know** How can you show respect for the rights of others?

② **Vocabulary** What is one **right** that you have?

③ **Activity** Act out some ways people can show respect for others.

④ **Cause and Effect** What may happen if you do not respect the rights of others?

Work and Play Together

Why It Matters   It is important to show respect for others when we do things together.

Learn

1 We **share** when we use something with others.

2 We show good **sportsmanship** when we play fairly.

3 We show respect for others by sharing and by playing fairly. When we do not agree, we listen to each person's ideas. Then we work together to find a solution.

Practice

Before   Think of something your class could do as a group.

During   Give everyone a chance to share ideas.

After   Talk about how well the people in your group worked together.

Apply

Make It Relevant   Work with a group to make up a game. Use what you have learned about working and playing together.

39

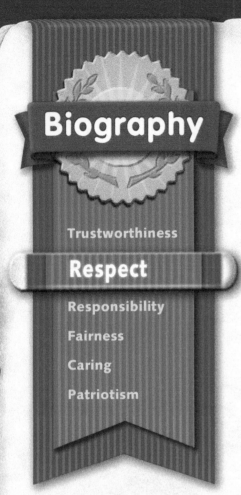

Trustworthiness

Respect

Responsibility

Fairness

Caring

Patriotism

Rosa Parks

Rosa Parks grew up in Alabama. At that time, many states had different rules for African Americans and white people. Parks worked to help win respect and rights for African Americans.

In 1955, Rosa Parks was riding the bus home from work. The bus driver asked her to give up her seat to a white man. Parks thought this was unfair. She did not get up, and she was arrested.

Why Character Counts

✎ How did Rosa Parks fight for respect for African Americans?

Rosa Parks believed in equal rights for all.

40

Rosa Parks refused to give up her seat on the bus.

African Americans in Montgomery, Alabama, did not ride city buses for 382 days. In 1964, the United States government made a law that gave African Americans the same rights as white people. Rosa Parks kept on working for rights for African Americans. In 1999, she was given the Congressional Gold Medal by President Clinton.

GO
ONLINE

For more resources, go to
www.harcourtschool.com/ss1

Time

1913
Born

2005
Died

1955 Does not give
up her seat on the bus

1999 Gets the
Congressional
Gold Medal

41

Fun Town Walk

Police Station

SCHOOL

Park Ranger

Police Officer

Teacher

CITY PARK

Find the citizens and leaders of Fun Town who are in the wrong places.

Fire Station

LIBRARY

CITY HALL

Principal

Mayor

MAYOR

Firefighter

Librarian

Online Adventures GO ONLINE

It is the first day of school!
Play an online game to help
Eco learn about rules and laws.
Play now, at www.harcourtschool.com/ss1

HARCOURT

ECO

Review and Test Prep

💡 **The Big Idea**

Citizenship Rules and laws guide people to live safely and be responsible citizens.

⭐ *Focus Skill* Cause and Effect

Copy and fill in the chart to show what you have learned about rules and responsibility.

Cause		Effect
Schools have rules.	→	Rules help people get along.

Cause		Effect
_____ _____	→	_____ _____

44

Write the word that goes with each meaning.

1 a person who lives in and belongs to a community

2 a rule that people in a community must follow

3 a choice that gets counted

4 an instruction that tells people how to act

5 a place where people live and work together

Word Bank

rule
(p. 10)

community
(p. 16)

citizen
(p. 16)

law
(p. 17)

vote
(p. 26)

☑ Facts and Main Ideas

6 Why do we have a responsibility to follow rules?

7 Who chooses leaders in a community?

8 Who leads the city government?

9 Which of these is a government service?

    A grocery store   **C** school

    B mall   **D** beach

10 What are Americans NOT free to do?

    A speak   **C** belong to groups

    B break laws   **D** worship

 Critical Thinking

⑪ What would happen if there were no laws in your community?

⑫ **Make It Relevant** What new rule would you make for your classroom? What makes this a good rule?

Skills

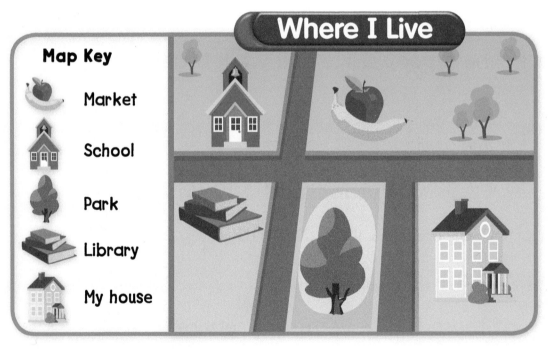

Where I Live

Map Key

🍎🍌 Market

🏫 School

🌳 Park

📚 Library

🏠 My house

⑬ How many places are shown on the map?

⑭ What symbol shows the school?

⑮ Where would you go to check out a book?

⑯ What is between my house and the library?

Skills

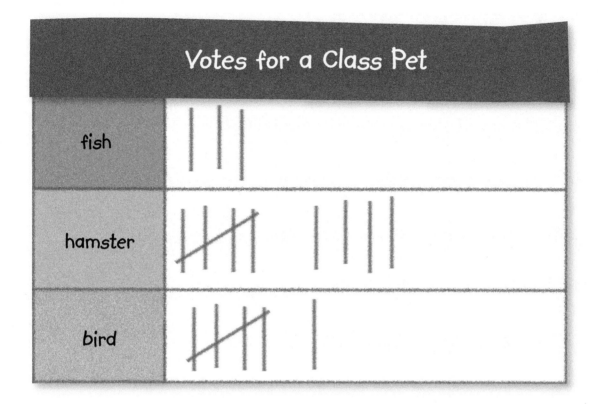

Votes for a Class Pet

fish				
hamster	|||| ||||			|||
bird	|||| ||	

17 How did the children in this class choose a pet?

18 Which pet did the class choose?

19 How many children voted for the bird?

20 Which pet got the fewest votes?

Activities

Show What You Know

Unit Writing Activity

Think About School Rules
A new child comes to your class. How will you help him or her learn the rules?

Write a List Write a list of school rules. Draw your classmates following each rule.

Unit Project

Campaign Rally Plan a campaign rally.

- Choose two people to run for Class Safety Monitor.
- Make posters and signs.
- Tell about safety rules at the rally.

Read More

The Child's World of Responsibility
by Nancy Pemberton

Know and Follow Rules
by Cheri J. Meiners

Voting
by Sarah De Capua

For more resources, go to www.harcourtschool.com/ss1

Marta for Safety Monitor

Where
People Live

The Big Idea

Places

People live in many different locations. Where people live affects the way they live.

What to Know

✔ How can a map help you find places?

✔ What kinds of land and water does the United States have?

✔ How does where people live affect their shelter and transportation?

✔ How do people use and save resources?

✔ How does weather affect people?

Where People Live

Talk About
Places

THE UNITED STATES OF AMERICA

" The United States is a big country with many kinds of places and people. "

" There are large cities along the Atlantic Ocean. "

" Many things grow in our country. "

Vocabulary

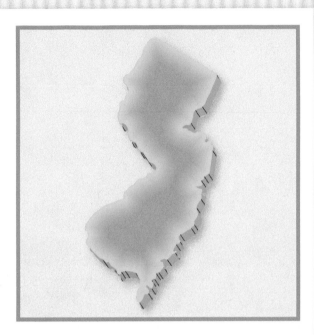

state   A part of a country.

(page 57)

country   An area of land with its own people and laws. (page 58)

globe A model of Earth. (page 60)

continent A large area of land. (page 60)

resource Anything that people can use. (page 74)

GO ONLINE For more resources, go to www.harcourtschool.com/ss1

Reading Social Studies

Focus Skill

Categorize and Classify

Why It Matters Categorizing and classifying helps you put information into groups.

Learn

- To categorize, put things into groups to show how they are the same.

- To classify, decide if something fits into a group.

Read the paragraphs.

Categorize
Classify

    The United States has many places to visit. People go to big cities such as New York City and Nashville. Families visit theme parks such as SeaWorld, Disneyland, and Six Flags.

    Other people visit national parks such as Grand Canyon National Park or Hot Springs National Park. Some visit historic places such as Fort McHenry or Boston Light.

Practice

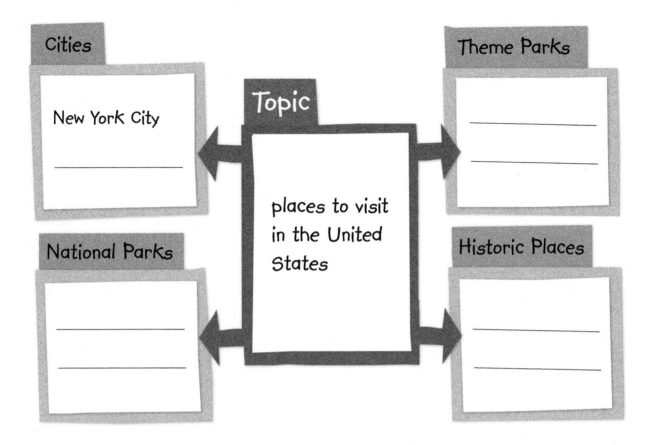

Cities

New York City
_____

Topic

places to visit
in the United
States

Theme Parks

_____
_____

National Parks

_____
_____
_____

Historic Places

_____
_____
_____

Copy this chart. Put each place that you read about into a group.

Apply

As you read, look for ways to categorize and classify other places in the United States.

Making Maps

by Elaine V. Emans

illustrated by Rob Dunlavey

I love to make maps!
I think it's great fun—
Making the boundaries,
And then, one by one,
Putting in railroads,
And each river bend,
And the tiny towns
Where little roads end.

I draw in mountains,
And often a lake,
And I've even had
Long bridges to make!
I like to do highways,
And when they are drawn
I dream that they take me
Where I've never gone.

Response Corner

1. **(Focus Skill) Categorize and Classify** What kinds of things can you find on a map?

2. **Make It Relevant** Draw a map of a place that you make up.

55

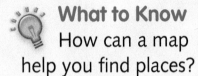
Finding Where You Are

What to Know
How can a map help you find places?

Vocabulary
location
state
country
border

 **Categorize and Classify**

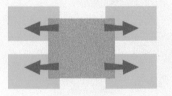

A **location** is the place where something is. This map shows the locations of places in a community.

MAP SKILL What places can you find on this map?

Maps can show many kinds of places.
One map may show streets in a city.
Another may show cities in a **state**.
Indiana is a state. Terre Haute is a city.

Cities in Indiana

MAP SKILL **Where is South Bend on this map?**

Some maps show states and countries. A **country** is an area of land with its own people and laws. The United States of America is our country. It has 50 states.

Lines on a map show borders. A **border** is where a state or country ends.

United States

CANADA

ALASKA

WASHINGTON

MONTANA

NORTH DAKOTA

MINNESOTA

NEW HAMPSHIRE
VERMONT
MAINE

OREGON

IDAHO

WYOMING

SOUTH DAKOTA

WISCONSIN

MICHIGAN

NEW YORK

MASSACHUSETTS
RHODE ISLAND

PENNSYLVANIA

CONNECTICUT
NEW JERSEY

NEVADA

UTAH

NEBRASKA

IOWA

INDIANA OHIO

WEST VIRGINIA

DELAWARE
MARYLAND
Washington, D.C.

ILLINOIS

CALIFORNIA

COLORADO

KANSAS

MISSOURI

KENTUCKY

VIRGINIA

NORTH CAROLINA

TENNESSEE

ARIZONA

NEW MEXICO

OKLAHOMA

ARKANSAS

SOUTH CAROLINA

PACIFIC OCEAN

GEORGIA

ALABAMA

MISSISSIPPI

TEXAS

ATLANTIC OCEAN

LOUISIANA

FLORIDA

HAWAII

MEXICO

Gulf of Mexico

MAP SKILL Find your state on this map.

58

Most maps use colors to show land and water. Green or brown shows land. Blue shows water. Rivers are blue lines on a map. Sometimes they are the borders of states.

MAP SKILL Name a city near a river.

Summary Maps show the locations of places such as streets, cities, states, countries, and rivers.

Review

❶ **What to Know** How can a map help you find places?

❷ **Vocabulary** What is a **country**?

❸ ✎ **Write** Look at a map. Write sentences that tell where you live.

❹ (Focus Skill) **Categorize and Classify** What is brown or green on a map? What is blue?

59

Use a Globe

Why It Matters   We live on **Earth**. You can use a globe to find places on Earth. A **globe** is a model of Earth.

Learn

A map is flat, but a globe is round. It shows what Earth looks like from space.

Like a map, a globe shows locations of places. Each large area of land is a **continent**. Each large body of water is an **ocean**.

Practice

1 Find and name the continent on which you live.

2 Use your finger to follow the border around South America.

3 Which ocean is between Australia and Africa?

Apply

Look at a globe. Find and name the seven continents and the five oceans.

For online activities, go to
www.harcourtschool.com/ss1

 What to Know
What kinds of land and water does the United States have?

Vocabulary
valley
plain

 **Categorize and Classify**

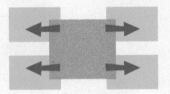

Land and Water

Different parts of the United States have different kinds of land. People can live near mountains, on hills, or in deserts.

hills

mountain

People also live in valleys. A **valley** is low land between mountains. Other people live on plains. A **plain** is land that is mostly flat. The land in most plains is good for growing food.

valley

desert

plain

The United States has many kinds of water. Many people live near water. Some live near lakes. Lakes can be large or small. Other people live near rivers. The water in rivers moves across the land to the ocean.

lake

river

The Atlantic Ocean and the Pacific Ocean are borders of the United States. Many people live near one of these oceans.

Summary The United States has many kinds of land and water.

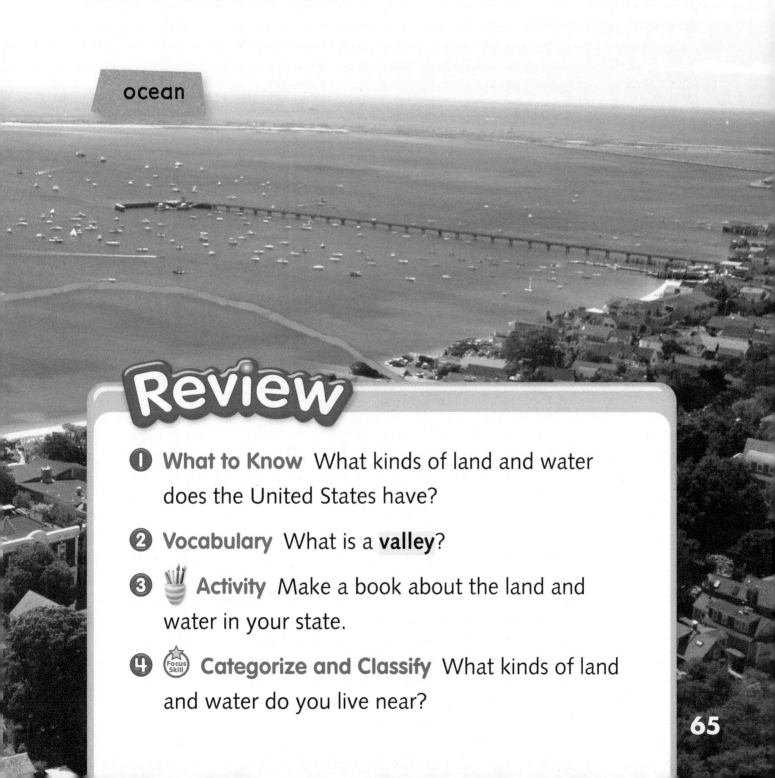

ocean

Review

1. **What to Know** What kinds of land and water does the United States have?

2. **Vocabulary** What is a **valley**?

3. **Activity** Make a book about the land and water in your state.

4. **Categorize and Classify** What kinds of land and water do you live near?

Field Trip

Read About

Great Smoky Mountains National Park is located on the border between North Carolina and Tennessee. In the forests of this park, visitors will see many kinds of plants and animals. They can also learn about the history of life in the Appalachian Mountains.

Find

United States

Great Smoky Mountains National Park

Great Smoky Mountains National Park

Great Smoky Mountains National Park has more than 800 miles of hiking trails.

At Cades Cove, visitors can see what life was like for early settlers in the Smokies.

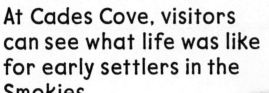

In the spring, many kinds of wildflowers bloom in the park.

About 600 black bears live in Great Smoky Mountains National Park.

A Virtual Tour

GO ONLINE
For more resources, go to
www.harcourtschool.com/ss1

People and Places

What to Know
How does where people live affect their shelter and transportation?

Vocabulary
neighborhood
farm
shelter
transportation

Focus Skill
Categorize and Classify

People live in many kinds of communities. A city is a large community with many neighborhoods. A **neighborhood** is a small part of a city.

Cleveland, Ohio

A town is a smaller community than a city. It has fewer people, stores, and streets.

Some communities are far away from towns and cities. Many people in these communities have farms. A **farm** is a place for growing plants and raising animals.

Hermann, Missouri

Farm near Fayetteville, Tennessee

Where people live affects the kind of shelter they have. A **shelter** is a home. Some people live in apartment buildings. Others live in houses.

Shelters

Children in History

Laura Ingalls Wilder

Laura Ingalls Wilder was a pioneer girl. She was born in a little log house in Wisconsin. Laura's family moved from place to place in a covered wagon. When Laura was older, she wrote books based on her childhood. These books helped young readers see what life was like for pioneers.

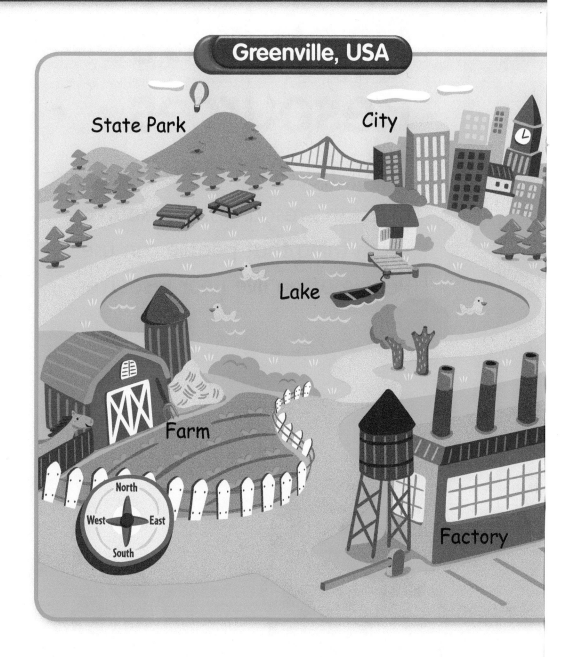

Greenville, USA

State Park

City

Lake

Farm

North
West East
South

Factory

Apply

Make It Relevant   Make a map of your classroom. Show directions.

For online activities, go to
www.harcourtschool.com/ss1

Transportation is any way of moving people and things from place to place. Transportation can be by land, water, or air.

Transportation

Summary   There are many kinds of communities. Where people live affects their shelter and transportation.

Review

❶ **What to Know** How does where people live affect their shelter and transportation?

❷ **Vocabulary** What is a **shelter**?

❸ **Activity** Draw a picture of the kind of community you live in.

❹ **Categorize and Classify** Make a chart showing kinds of transportation that go by land, by water, and by air.

Find Directions on a

Why It Matters **Directions** point the way to places. They help you find locations.

Learn

The four main directions are called **cardinal directions**. They are north, south, east, and west.

If you face north, west is on your left. East is on your right. South is behind you.

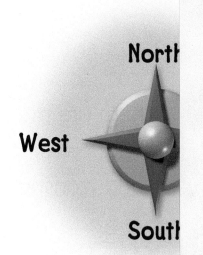

North

West

South

Practice

① What is east of the state park?

② What is north of the farm?

③ Find the city. Now move your finger to the factory. In which direction did you move?

Lesson  4

What to Know
How do people use and save resources?

Vocabulary
resource
recycle

Focus Skill
Categorize and Classify

People Use Resources

Soil, trees, and water are some of Earth's resources. A **resource** is anything that people can use. People often live near resources.

Much of the land on Earth is covered with soil. People use soil to grow food on farms. Many of the foods that you eat come from farms all over the country.

Foods

People grow some kinds of trees to get food. Fruits and nuts grow on trees. People also use wood from trees to make buildings and furniture.

All living things need water to live. People build dams to store water. People who live near water often fish for food.

It is our responsibility to take care of Earth's resources. We can keep our land and water clean. We can plant trees to take the place of trees that are cut down.

NET WT.
7.09 g.

SUNFLOWER
Mammoth

Edible
Seeds

We can also **recycle**, or make something old into something new. You can recycle plastic bags, paper, cans, and glass.

Summary People use many resources. We should take care of Earth's resources.

Review

❶ **What to Know** How do people use and save resources?

❷ **Vocabulary** How can we **recycle**?

❸ ✏️ **Write** Write sentences that tell how you use resources.

❹ ⭐ **Categorize and Classify** List some paper, plastic, and glass things you can recycle.

Build Vocabulary

Why It Matters   As you read, you will come to many new words. You can write these words in a web to help you learn them.

Learn

The word web on this page shows how words about conservation were grouped. Copy the web.

● What word is in the middle?

● Why is <u>water</u> in one of the other boxes?

conservation

water

Practice

Read the paragraph. Which words name things we can conserve? Add these words to your word web.

Conservation is the saving of resources to make them last longer. We can conserve water by turning it off when we brush our teeth. We can conserve trees by using less paper. We can also conserve gasoline by not driving our cars as much.

Apply

Make It Relevant Make a web for the word **recycle**. Add words to your web that tell about **recycling**.

Trustworthiness

Respect

Responsibility

Fairness

Caring

Patriotism

Why Character Counts

✎ How did George Washington Carver show that he cared about farmers?

George Washington Carver

As a young boy, George Washington Carver cared about plants. His nickname was "the plant doctor." "I wanted to know the name of every stone and flower and insect and bird and beast," he said. Carver went to school to learn about plants and farming. He became a teacher to help farmers.

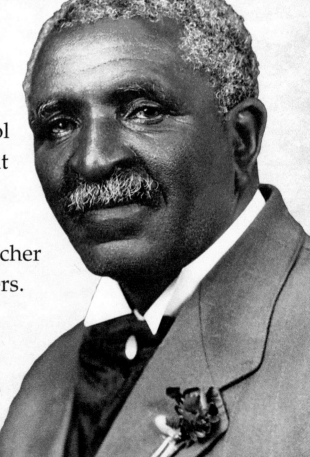

George Washington Carver was an inventor and a teacher.

George Washington Carver has appeared on postage stamps.

George Washington Carver found more than three hundred uses for peanuts.

Many farmers grew only cotton. This made the soil poor. Carver taught the farmers that growing peanuts can help make the soil healthy so other crops can grow. Carver found many ways to use peanuts. They can be made into peanut butter, soap, glue, and paint.

For more resources, go to
www.harcourtschool.com/ss1

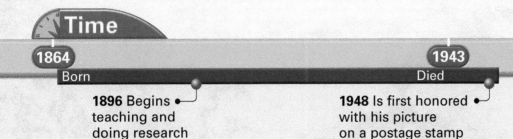

Time

1864
Born

1943
Died

1896 Begins teaching and doing research

1948 Is first honored with his picture on a postage stamp

What to Know
How does weather affect people?

Vocabulary

weather

season

recreation

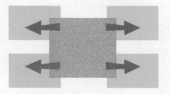 **Categorize and Classify**

What's the Weather?

There are many kinds of weather. **Weather** is the way the air feels outside.

Weather changes with the seasons. A **season** is a time of year. The four seasons are spring, summer, fall, and winter. A season's weather is different in different places.

Spring

Summer

Fall

Winter

People check the weather before they decide what to wear. They choose clothes that will keep them warm, dry, or cool.

Fast Fact!

The hottest place in the United States is a desert in California called Death Valley. One time, it was 134 degrees in Death Valley!

People also choose their recreation to go with the weather. **Recreation** is what people do for fun. Playing sports or games and enjoying the outdoors are kinds of recreation.

Summary There are many kinds of weather. The weather affects how we dress and how we play.

Review

1. **What to Know** How does weather affect people?

2. **Vocabulary** What are the four **seasons**?

3. 🖌 **Activity** Be a weather reporter. Tell people what clothes to wear for each kind of weather you report.

4. ⭐(Focus Skill) **Categorize and Classify** Make a chart that shows ways to have fun in summer and in winter.

Points of View

The Sidewalk Reporter asks:
"What is special about the place where you live?"

Eddie

"I can swim at the beach in summer and ski in the mountains in winter."

Mrs. Johnson

"People come from all over to see our beautiful butterflies."

View from the Past

Daniel Boone: Wilderness Road

Daniel Boone liked to explore. He found lands in Kentucky that were good for farming and hunting. In 1775, he led groups of settlers to these lands on the Wilderness Road.

Ms. Patel

"We have hundreds of places to eat that have foods of every kind."

Mr. Ruiz

"I catch fish in the many lakes and rivers near our community."

Erin

"We have a good bus system. It makes it easy to get around the community."

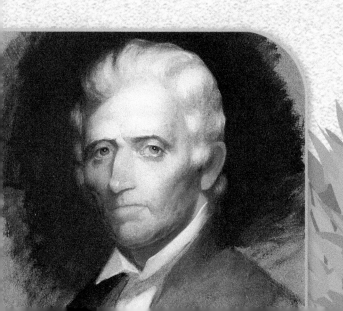

It's Your Turn

- Does your community have any of these special things? If so, which ones?
- What makes your community special?

Read the clues.

Find the answers in the picture. Some clues have more than one answer.

I live on a farm.

I am a shelter for animals.

I am a kind of weather.

I am a resource.

I am a kind of recreation.

I am a season.

I am a kind of transportation.

Online GO ONLINE **Adventures**

How can you get from school to the playground? Play the online game with Eco. Play now, at www.harcourtschool.com/ss1

Review and Test Prep

The Big Idea

Places People live in many different locations.
Where people live affects the way they live.

⭐ (Focus Skill) Categorize and Classify

Copy and fill in the chart to categorize and
classify clothing for different kinds of weather.

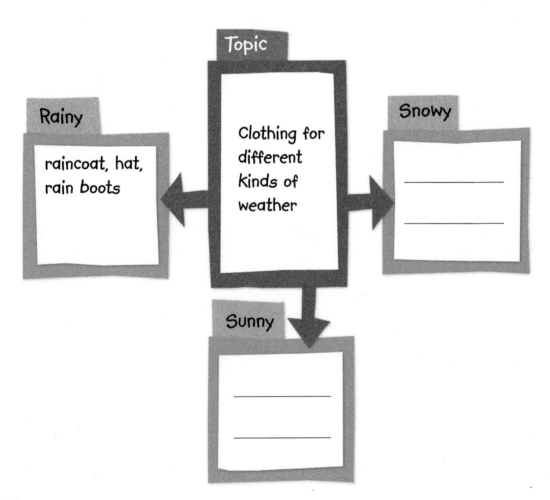

Topic

Clothing for different kinds of weather

Rainy
raincoat, hat, rain boots

Snowy
_____
_____

Sunny
_____
_____

Vocabulary

Write the word that goes with each picture.

1. _____

2. _____

3. Africa _____

4. New Jersey _____

5. United States _____

Word Bank

state
(p. 57)

country
(p. 58)

globe
(p. 60)

continent
(p. 60)

resource
(p. 74)

Facts and Main Ideas

6. What does a border show?

7. What kinds of land and water do people live near?

8. How is a city different from a town?

9. Which resource do people use to fish for food?

   A soil   **C** rocks

   B trees   **D** water

10. Which is NOT a kind of recreation you would do at the beach?

   A swimming   **C** ice-skating

   B volleyball   **D** sailing

☑ Critical Thinking

⑪ How are cities, towns, and farms alike and different?

⑫ **Make It Relevant** What would your life be like if you lived where it snowed a lot?

☑ Skills

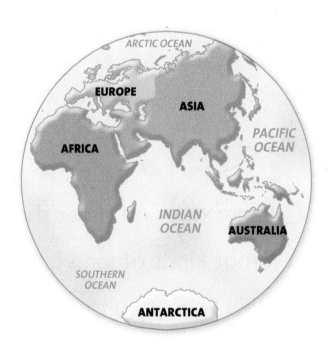

⑬ How many continents are there?

⑭ Name the five oceans.

⑮ On which continent do you live?

⑯ Which oceans lie around Australia?

Zoo

17 What is west of the lions?

18 What is north of the elephants?

19 From the tigers, in which direction are the dolphins?

20 Move your finger from the gorillas to the tigers. In which direction did you move?

Activities

Show What You Know

 **Unit Writing Activity**

Tell About a Place What words could you use to tell a pen pal about where you live?

Write a Letter Write a short letter to your pen pal telling about where you live.

 Unit Project

Places We Live Mural Create a mural to show where you live.

- Think about different things in your community.
- Draw them on a mural.
- Share it with another class.

Read More

Rand McNally

Coast to Coast
by Marcia S. Freeman

Candlewick Press, Inc.

The Once Upon a Time Map Book
by B.G. Hennessy

Aladdin

The Year at Maple Hill Farm
by Alice and Martin Provensen

GO ONLINE For more resources, go to www.harcourtschool.com/ss1

We Love Our Country

The Big Idea

Our Country

We learn about our country through its symbols, heroes, and holidays.

What to Know

✔ What are the Declaration of Independence and the United States Constitution?

✔ What is the Pledge of Allegiance?

✔ Why are our country's symbols important?

✔ Why do we have national holidays?

We Love Our Country

Talk About

Our Country

" We honor our country on special days. "

" Our country has many important symbols. "

" We remember our heroes. "

97

flag A piece of cloth with colors and shapes that stand for things. (page 116)

freedom The right people have to make their own choices.

(page 108)

landmark   A symbol that is a place people can visit.

(page 122)

national holiday   A day to honor a person or an event that is important to our country. (page 128)

hero   A person who does something brave or important to help others. (page 129)

GO
ONLINE
For more resources, go to
www.harcourtschool.com/ss1

Reading Social Studies

(Focus Skill) # Main Idea and Details

Why It Matters Finding the main idea and details helps you understand what you are reading about.

Learn

● The main idea tells you what you are reading about. It is the most important part.

● A detail gives more information. The details explain the main idea.

Read the paragraph.

Main Idea
The United States has many symbols that show that Americans are free. The bald eagle

Detail
is one symbol of our country. It is a strong bird that flies free. We keep the Declaration of Independence and the Constitution of the United States in special places. These symbols show how hard our first leaders worked to make our country free.

Practice

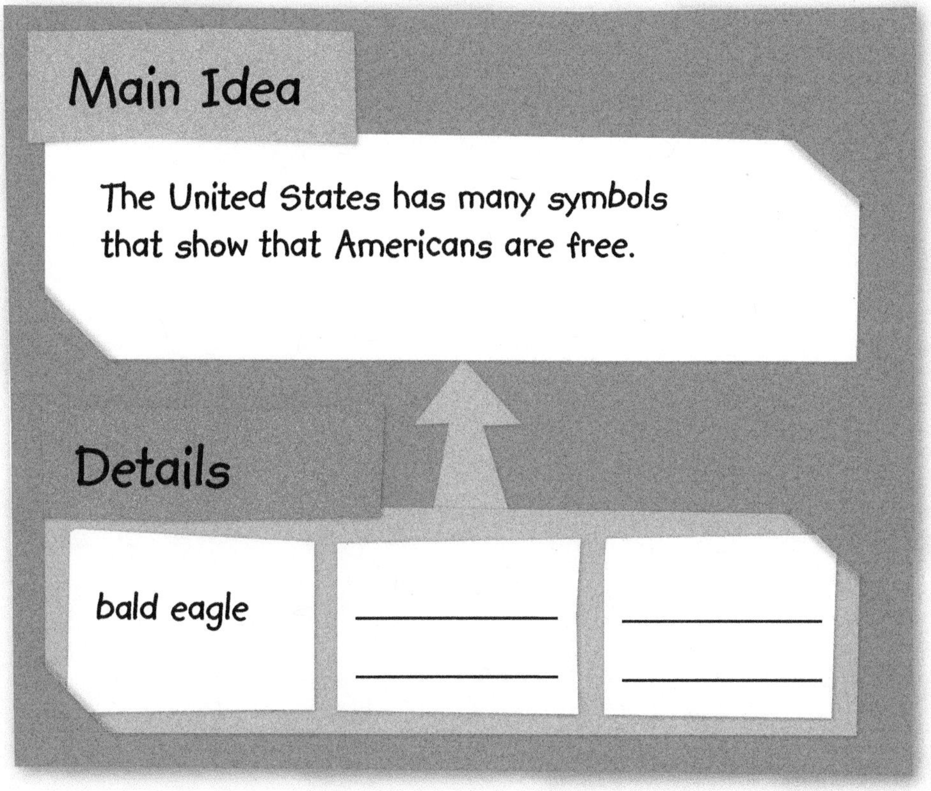

Main Idea
The United States has many symbols that show that Americans are free.

Details

bald eagle	_____ _____	_____ _____

This chart shows the main idea and one detail from what you just read. What details could you add? Copy the chart and fill it in.

Apply

As you read, look for the main idea and details in each lesson.

America

by Samuel F. Smith

illustrated by Richard Johnson

My country, 'tis of thee,
Sweet land of liberty,
Of thee I sing.
Land where my fathers died,
Land of the Pilgrims' pride,
From every mountainside
Let freedom ring!

My native country, thee,
Land of the noble free,
Thy name I love.
I love thy rocks and rills,
Thy woods and templed hills;
My heart with rapture thrills
Like that above.

Response Corner

1. **Main Idea and Details** What does the author love about America?

2. **Make It Relevant** How does this song make you feel?

Vocabulary
settler
colony
freedom

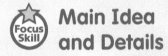
Main Idea
and Details

Our Country Begins

More than four hundred years ago, settlers sailed to North America from countries in Europe. A **settler** is a person who makes a home in a new place.

MAP SKILL What ocean did the <u>Mayflower</u> cross?

One group of settlers was the Pilgrims. They sailed from England on a ship called the <u>Mayflower</u>. The Pilgrims built a village in a place called Plymouth.

Wampanoag People lived in the place where the Pilgrims landed. They showed the Pilgrims how to grow corn.

The English king called the Pilgrims' land a **colony** of England. This meant that the land was ruled by England.

By 1732, there were 13 English colonies in North America. The people living in the colonies had to follow England's laws. Many people thought the laws were not fair.

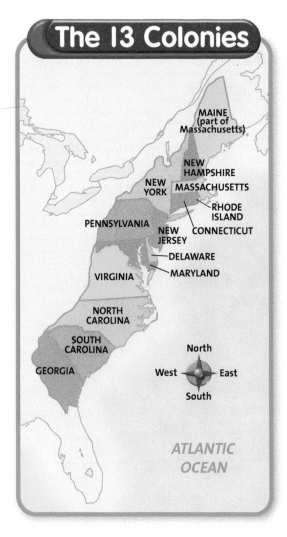

The 13 Colonies

MAINE
(part of
Massachusetts)

NEW
HAMPSHIRE

NEW
YORK   MASSACHUSETTS

RHODE
ISLAND

PENNSYLVANIA

NEW   CONNECTICUT
JERSEY

DELAWARE

MARYLAND

VIRGINIA

NORTH
CAROLINA

SOUTH
CAROLINA   North

GEORGIA   West   East

South

ATLANTIC
OCEAN

MAP SKILL On what ocean were the colonies?

Independence Hall in
Philadelphia, Pennsylvania

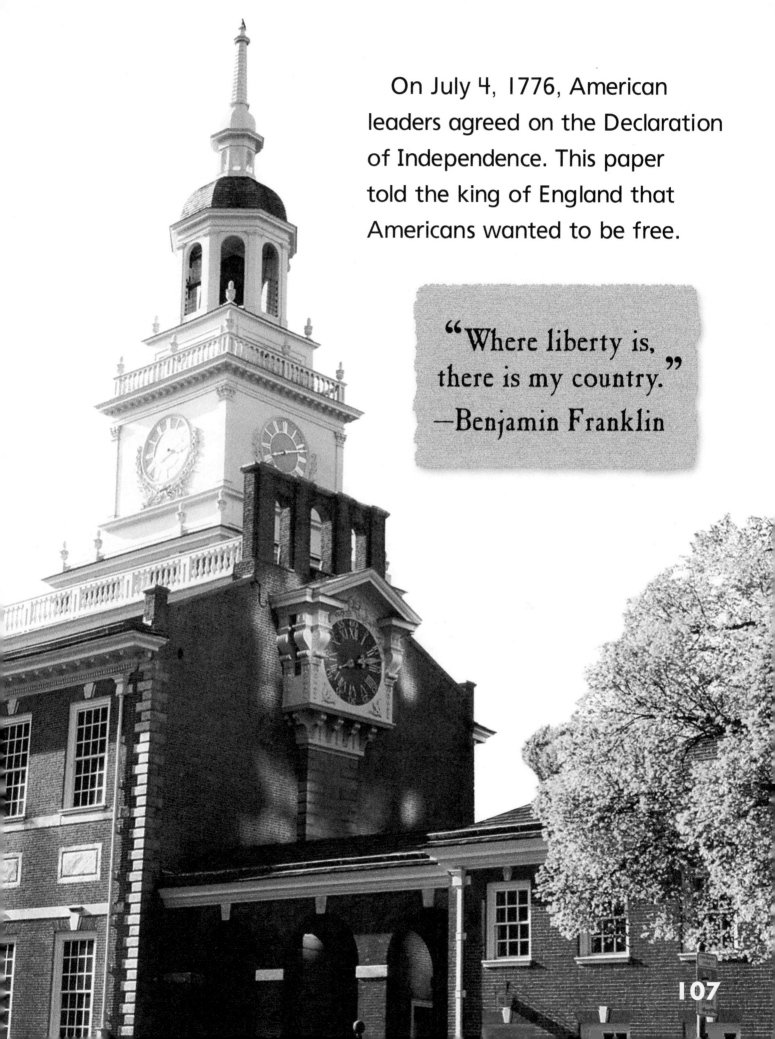

On July 4, 1776, American leaders agreed on the Declaration of Independence. This paper told the king of England that Americans wanted to be free.

"Where liberty is, there is my country."
—Benjamin Franklin

Americans fought a war with England to get their freedom. **Freedom** is the right to make choices. General George Washington led many battles against English soldiers. He helped Americans win the war.

Tricorn hat

108

After the war, the 13 colonies became the United States of America. American leaders wrote the United States Constitution. The Constitution is the set of rules for our country. George Washington became the first President of the United States.

First Lady
Martha Washington

Summary The Declaration of Independence and the United States Constitution are important symbols of our freedom.

Review

1. **What to Know** What are the Declaration of Independence and the United States Constitution?

2. **Vocabulary** Who ruled the **colonies** in North America?

3. **Write** Explain why American leaders wrote the Constitution.

4. **Main Idea and Details** Why did Americans fight a war with England?

Trustworthiness

Respect

Responsibility

Fairness

Caring

Patriotism

Why Character Counts

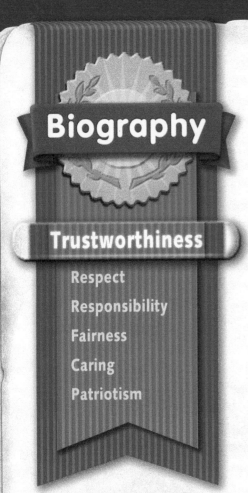

✎ **Why do you think people trusted George Washington?**

George Washington

George Washington thought that people should work hard and be honest. He started working when he was 17 years old. He helped people make maps of their land. He was so honest and fair that many people wanted him to work for them. Later, Washington joined the army and became a trusted leader.

George Washington was the first President of the United States.

As a young man, Washington owned and worked with land.

Washington was a kind and fair leader. He rewarded people for their hard work.

Washington led Americans in a fight to be free and to rule their own country. When the United States began, Americans chose him to be their first President.

GO ONLINE For more resources, go to **www.harcourtschool.com/ss1**

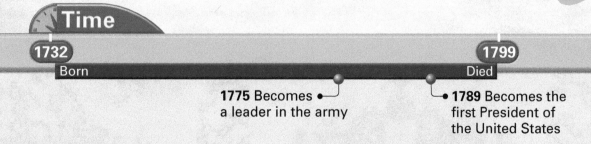

Time

| 1732 | | | | 1799 |
| Born | | | | Died |

1775 Becomes a leader in the army

1789 Becomes the first President of the United States

Learning About Freedom

You can learn about the birth of our country from things that were made at that time. Maps, papers, and works of art show the ideas and feelings people had when they were starting the United States of America.

DBQ ❶ What can you learn by reading someone's letters?

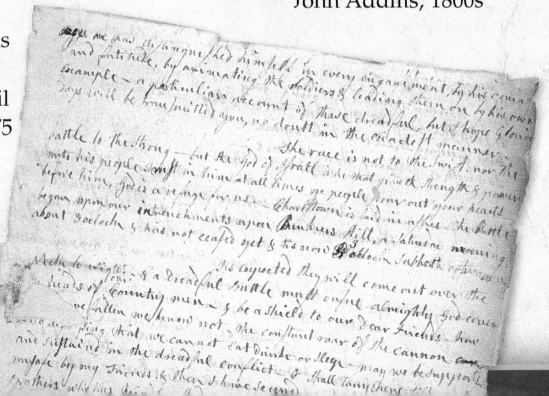

Painting of John Adams, 1800s

A letter to John Adams from his wife Abigail Adams, 1775

DBQ ❷ What do this map and this drawing tell you about our country long ago?

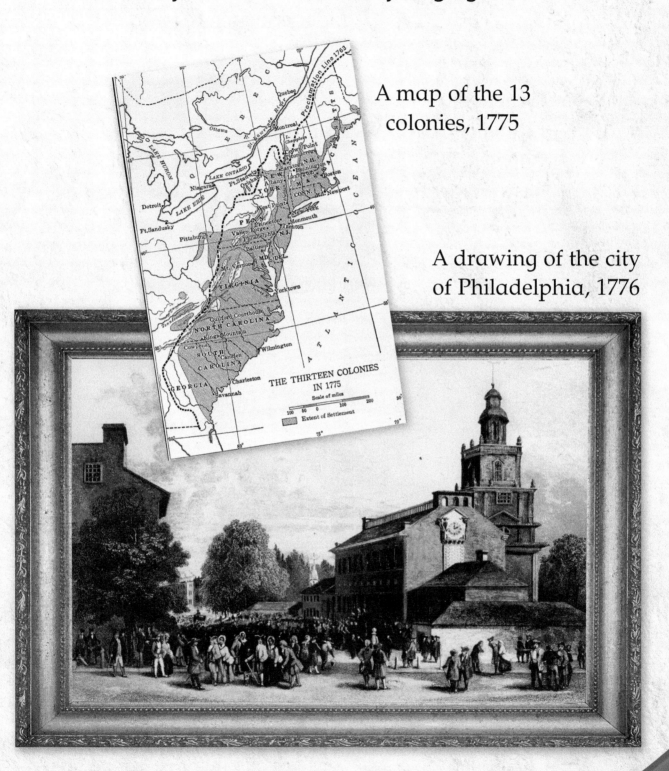

A map of the 13 colonies, 1775

A drawing of the city of Philadelphia, 1776

THE THIRTEEN COLONIES IN 1775

DBQ ③ What do the names at the bottom of the Declaration of Independence tell you?

The room where the Declaration of Independence was signed

The Declaration of Independence

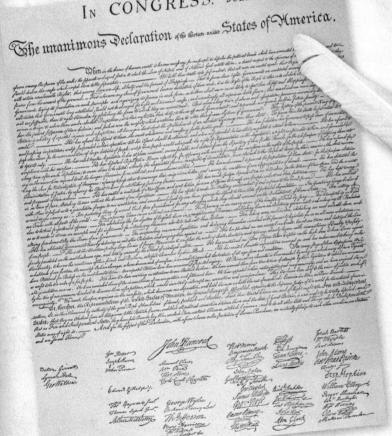

Pen and ink set used by the signers

DBQ ④ What do the words "We the People . . ." tell you about the rules and laws in the Constitution?

George Washington helped write the Constitution

The United States Constitution

✎ Write About It

What do things from our history tell us about freedom?

I Pledge Allegiance

What to Know
What is
the Pledge of
Allegiance?

Vocabulary
flag
pledge

 **Main Idea and Details**

The American flag is a symbol of our country. A **flag** is a piece of cloth with colors and shapes that stand for things. States have their own flags. Some groups also have flags.

Flags

Our flag is red, white, and blue. It has 50 stars. Each star stands for one of the states in our country. The 13 stripes stand for the first 13 states. Our flag changed as our country grew.

1777

1820

1960

Each morning, we face the flag and say the Pledge of Allegiance. A **pledge** is a kind of promise.

The Pledge of Allegiance

I pledge allegiance to the Flag
of the United States of America,
and to the Republic
for which it stands,
one Nation under God, indivisible,
with liberty and justice for all.

The pledge reminds us about being good citizens. When we say the pledge, we promise to respect the flag and our country.

Fast Fact!

In 1814, Francis Scott Key saw a flag still flying after a long battle. He wrote a poem about it called "The Star-Spangled Banner." It is now our country's song.

Summary The Pledge of Allegiance is a promise we make to respect the flag and our country.

Review

1. **What to Know** What is the Pledge of Allegiance?

2. **Vocabulary** Where have you seen our country's **flag**?

3. ✏️ **Write** Write sentences that tell what our country's flag looks like.

4. 🌟(Focus Skill) **Main Idea and Details** What does the American flag stand for?

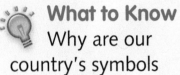
American Symbols

The United States of America has many symbols. These symbols stand for events, people, and ideas that are important to us.

 What to Know
Why are our country's symbols important?

Vocabulary
landmark

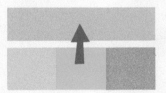 **Main Idea and Details**

Liberty Bell

Some symbols are plants or animals. The rose and the bald eagle are American symbols.

Symbols can also be objects. Our country's flag is a symbol. The pictures on our money are symbols, too.

Bald Eagle

Some symbols are places that we can visit. These symbols are called **landmarks**.

Washington Monument

Capitol

Mount Rushmore

Gateway Arch

Summary Our country has symbols that stand for people, events, and ideas that are important to us.

Review

1. **What to Know** Why are our country's symbols important?

2. **Vocabulary** What is one **landmark** in our country?

3. **Activity** Make a mobile that shows some of our country's symbols.

4. **Main Idea and Details** What bird is an American symbol?

123

Read a Diagram

Why It Matters   A **diagram** is a picture that shows the parts of something.

Learn

The picture on the next page is a diagram of the Statue of Liberty. The statue shows a woman who stands for freedom.

Practice

❶ What is the woman holding up high?

❷ How many windows are in her crown?

❸ What is the woman wearing?

❹ What is the name of the island the statue is on?

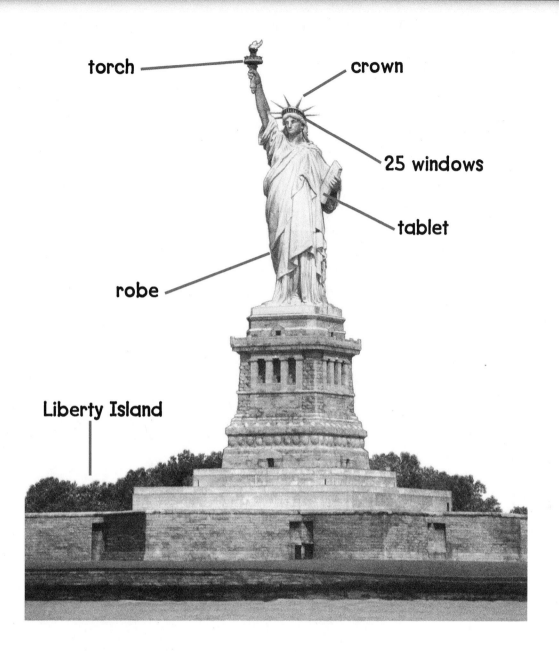

torch — crown

25 windows

tablet

robe

Liberty Island

Apply

Make a diagram of another American landmark or symbol. Name the parts.

GO
ONLINE

For online activities, go to
www.harcourtschool.com/ss1

Field Trip

Read About

The Liberty Bell is a symbol of freedom. People can see the Liberty Bell at Independence National Historical Park in Philadelphia, Pennsylvania. People visit the park to learn about how our nation was formed. The buildings in the park show the history of the United States of America.

Find

United States

Philadelphia, Pennsylvania

The Liberty Bell

The Liberty Bell rang for the last time in 1846 for George Washington's birthday celebration.

Flags from all 50 states are on display at the National Constitution Center.

The Declaration of Independence and the United States Constitution were signed at Independence Hall.

Visitors can view the Declaration of Independence.

Reenactors at Franklin Court teach visitors about the life of Benjamin Franklin.

A Virtual Tour

GO ONLINE For more resources, go to www.harcourtschool.com/ss1

What to Know
Why do we have
national holidays?

Vocabulary
national holiday
hero

**Main Idea
and Details**

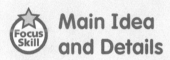

Holidays and Heroes

A **national holiday** is a day to honor a person or an event that is important to our country. Memorial Day and Veterans Day are two national holidays. On these days, we remember people who have helped in our country's wars.

A **hero** is a person who does something brave or important to help others. Men and women who work in the military are heroes. They help protect our country.

Army

Navy

Marines

Our country has many heroes. We have holidays to honor them. Dr. Martin Luther King, Jr., Day honors a leader who helped all Americans have the same rights.

Presidents' Day started as George Washington's Birthday. It was a holiday to remember our first President. Now it is a day to remember the work of all our Presidents.

Dr. Martin Luther King, Jr.

Abraham Lincoln

George Washington

Some holidays honor something important that happened in our country. Long ago, the Pilgrims were thankful for a good harvest. They shared a feast with the Wampanoag Indians. We remember that feast with a holiday called Thanksgiving.

Thanksgiving, 1621

Giving thanks today

July 4 is Independence Day, our country's birthday. Many communities have parades and fireworks on this day.

Constitution Day honors the day when American leaders signed the United States Constitution. On this day, we learn more about our Constitution.

Labor Day is a day to honor the workers of our country. Many people do not work on this holiday. They spend the day relaxing and having picnics.

Summary National holidays help us remember the important events and heroes of our country.

Review

1. **What to Know** Why do we have national holidays?

2. **Vocabulary** Name an American **hero**.

3. **Activity** With your class, make a chart about our country's national holidays.

4. **Main Idea and Details** What do Americans do on national holidays?

Read a Calendar

Why It Matters   A **calendar** is used to show time.

Learn

A calendar shows days, weeks, and months. A week has 7 days. A year has 365 days. It also has 52 weeks and 12 months.

Today means this day. **Yesterday** is the day before today. **Tomorrow** is the day after today.

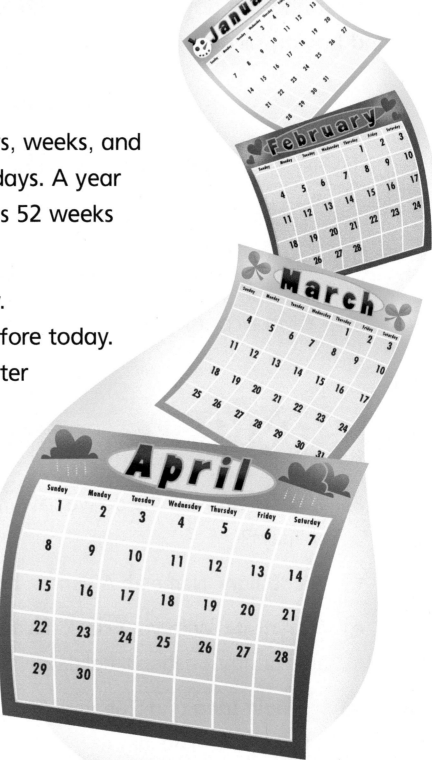

February

Sunday	Monday	Tuesday	Wednesday	Thursday	Friday	Saturday
				1	2	3
4 Rosa Parks's Birthday	5	6	7	8	9	10
11 Thomas Edison's Birthday	12 Lincoln's Birthday	13	14	15 Susan B. Anthony's Birthday	16	17
18	19 Presidents' Day	20	21	22 Washington's Birthday	23	24
25	26	27	28			

Practice

1 What month does this page show?

2 How many days are there in this month?

3 Name the birthdays in February. On what day of the week is each birthday?

Apply

Find today, tomorrow, and yesterday on a calendar.

GO ONLINE For online activities, go to www.harcourtschool.com/ss1

Flag Day

Bernard J. Cigrand was a teacher who lived more than 100 years ago. He loved the American flag. He put it on his desk, where the children in his class could see it. He asked them to write about how the flag made them feel.

Cigrand and others wanted to have a national holiday to honor our flag. They worked for this idea for many years. At last, in 1949, the government made the holiday they wanted. June 14 became Flag Day.

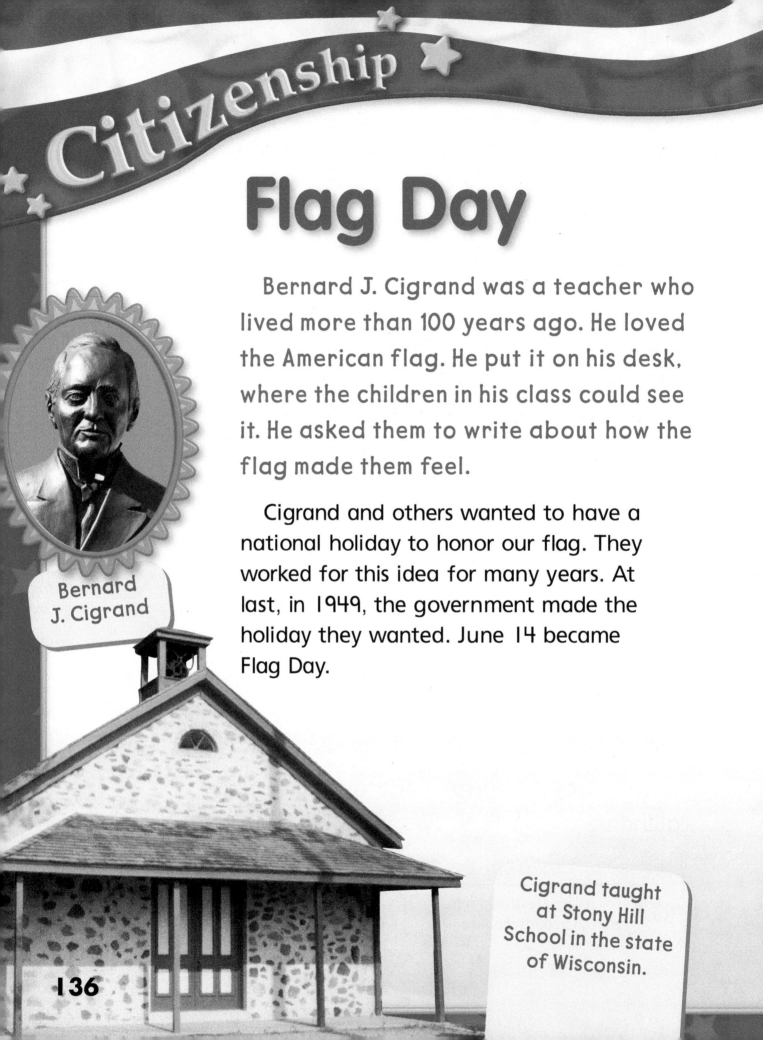

Bernard J. Cigrand

Cigrand taught at Stony Hill School in the state of Wisconsin.

You can see the flag in many places. Some people hang the flag on a flagpole. This is called flying the flag. People fly flags at home and at work. The flag flies at your school, too.

Sometimes, the flag flies halfway up the flagpole. This happens when someone important to our country has died. Flying the flag this way shows respect for the person.

Make It Relevant How do you feel about the flag?

Find what's hidden.

Can you find the eight symbols and landmarks hidden in the picture?

Symbols

flag

dollar bill

bald eagle

penny

Landmarks

Liberty Bell

Statue of Liberty

Washington Monument

U.S. Capitol

Online Adventures **GO ONLINE**

It is time for a holiday party! Play the online game to help Eco plan everything. Play now, at www.harcourtschool.com/ss1

Review and Test Prep ✓

💡 The Big Idea

Our Country We learn about our country through its symbols, heroes, and holidays.

⭐ Main Idea and Details

Copy and fill in the chart to show what you learned about the Pledge of Allegiance.

Main Idea

The Pledge of Allegiance reminds us about being good citizens.

Details

We face the flag when we say the pledge. | _____ _____ | _____ _____

✓ Vocabulary

Write the word that completes each sentence.

Word Bank

freedom
(p. 108)

flag
(p. 116)

landmark
(p. 122)

national
holiday
(p. 128)

hero
(p. 129)

1 The Washington Monument is a _____.

2 The Fourth of July is a _____.

3 The red and white stripes on our
_____ stand for the first 13 states.

4 Americans fought a war with England to
have _____, or the right to make choices.

5 Dr. Martin Luther King, Jr., is a _____.

✓ Facts and Main Ideas

6 Who were the Pilgrims?

7 Why did Americans fight a war with England?

8 What do the 50 stars on the American flag stand for?

9 Which of these symbols is a landmark?

    A flag   **C** rose

    B Mount Rushmore   **D** bald eagle

10 Which is NOT a national holiday?

    A Veterans Day   **C** Work Day

    B Labor Day   **D** Independence Day

 Critical Thinking

11 Why do we celebrate national holidays?

12 **Make It Relevant** How would your life be different if we did not have the United States Constitution?

Skills

13 How many days are in January?

14 When do we honor Dr. Martin Luther King, Jr.?

15 What is special about January 1?

16 On what day of the week is Benjamin Franklin's birthday?

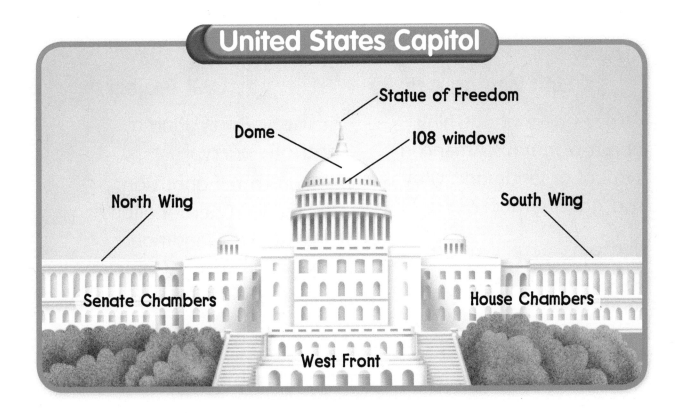

⑰ What is on top of the dome?

⑱ What is the front of the Capitol building called?

⑲ How many windows are in the dome?

⑳ Which chambers are in the South Wing?

Unit 3 Activities

Show What You Know

 Unit Writing Activity

Choose a Symbol Think about a famous American symbol or landmark. Why is it a good symbol?

Write a Poem Write a poem about the symbol or landmark.

 Unit Project

Patriotic Party Plan a patriotic party.

- Plan to tell about an American hero, holiday, symbol, or landmark.
- Make invitations and classroom decorations.

Read More

Flag Day
by Mari C. Schuh

The Story of "The Star-Spangled Banner"
by Patricia A. Pingry

George Washington's Breakfast
by Jean Fritz

GO ONLINE For more resources, go to www.harcourtschool.com/ss1

144

Our Changing World

The Big Idea

Change

In many ways, people today are the same as people who lived long ago. But the way people live has changed over time.

What to Know

✔ How are the lives of people today different from the lives of people long ago? How are they the same?

✔ What were schools like long ago?

✔ What can happen to communities over time?

✔ How has transportation changed over time?

Our Changing World

Unit 4

Talk About

Change

"Long ago, schools were different."

" The tools we use have
changed over time. "

" Technology has made
transportation better. "

past   The time before now.

(page 178)

present   The time now.

(page 179)

146

change To become different. (page 170)

technology All of the tools we use to make our lives easier. (page 186)

0 1 2 3 4

time line A line that shows the order in which things have happened. (page 182)

GO ONLINE For more resources, go to www.harcourtschool.com/ss1

Reading Social Studies

Focus Skill

Sequence

Why It Matters Knowing the sequence, or order, of things helps you understand what you read.

Learn

● Sequence is the order in which things happen. What happens first? What happens next? What happens last?

● Look for sequence words such as <u>first</u>, <u>next</u>, <u>then</u>, <u>later</u>, <u>last</u>, and <u>finally</u>.

Read the paragraph.

Long ago, the school day was not like your school day. Children walked to school. All the

Sequence grades shared one classroom. First, they all read out loud. Next, each grade was called up for a lesson while the other children worked quietly. Last, the children helped the teacher do chores. They cleaned the classroom and got wood for the fire.

Practice

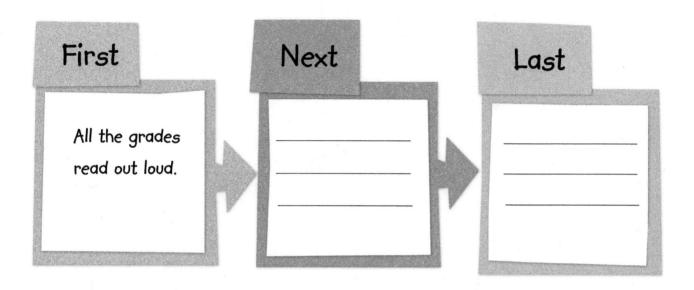

First

All the grades
read out loud.

Next

_____
_____
_____

Last

_____
_____
_____

This chart shows the sequence of things
that happened on a school day long ago.
Copy the chart and fill in the next things
in order.

Apply

As you read, look for words that tell
the sequence of things.

Aunt Flossie's Hats
(and Crab Cakes Later)

by Elizabeth Fitzgerald Howard

paintings by James Ransome

On Sunday afternoons,
Sarah and I go to see
Great-great-aunt Flossie.
Sarah and I love
Aunt Flossie's house.
It is crowded full of stuff
and things.
Books and pictures and
lamps and pillows…

Plates and trays and old
dried flowers…
And boxes
and boxes
and boxes
of HATS!

On Sunday afternoons when Sarah and I
go to see Aunt Flossie, she says,
"Come in, Susan. Come in, Sarah.
Have some tea. Have some cookies.
Later we can get some crab cakes!"

We sip our tea and eat our cookies,
and then Aunt Flossie lets us look
in her hatboxes.

We pick out hats and try them on.
Aunt Flossie says they are her memories,
and each hat has its story.

One Sunday afternoon, I picked out
a wooly winter hat, sort of green, maybe.
Aunt Flossie thought a minute.
Aunt Flossie almost always thinks a minute
before she starts a hat story.
Then she sniffed the wooly hat.
"Just a little smoky smell now," she said.
Sarah and I sniffed the hat, too.
"Smoky smell, Aunt Flossie?"

"The big fire," Aunt Flossie said.
"The big fire in Baltimore.
Everything smelled of smoke for miles around.
For days and days.
Big fire. Didn't come near our house
on Centre Street, but we could hear
fire engines racing down St. Paul.

Horses' hooves clattering.
Bells! Whistles!
Your great-grandma and I couldn't sleep.
We grabbed our coats and hats and ran outside.
Worried about Uncle Jimmy's grocery store,
worried about the terrapins and crabs.
Big fire in Baltimore."

Aunt Flossie closed her eyes.
I think she was seeing long ago.
I wondered about crab cakes.
Did they have crab cakes way back then?
Then Sarah sniffed Aunt Flossie's hat.
"No more smoky smell," she said.
But I thought I could smell some,
just a little.

"I like that story," I said.

"So do I," said Sarah.

"Crab cakes!" said Aunt Flossie.

"What a wonderful idea! Sarah, Susan,
telephone your parents.
We'll go get some crab cakes right now!"

I think Sarah and I will always agree
about one thing: Nothing in the whole wide
world tastes as good as crab cakes.

But crab cakes taste best after stories...
stories about Aunt Flossie's hats!

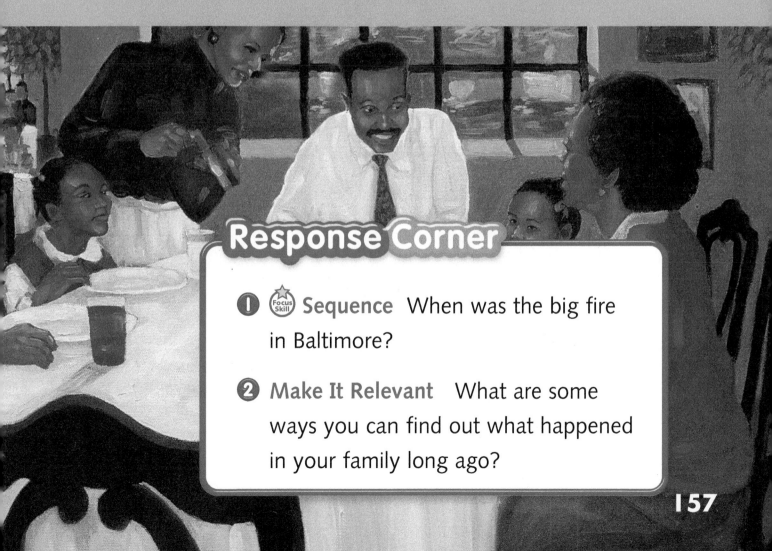

Response Corner

1. **Focus Skill** **Sequence** When was the big fire
   in Baltimore?

2. **Make It Relevant** What are some
   ways you can find out what happened
   in your family long ago?

People Long Ago

What to Know

What to Know
How are the lives of people today different from the lives of people long ago? How are they the same?

Vocabulary
communication

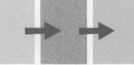

Sequence

Darla loves to watch home movies with Grandma Mary. Darla learns what life was like when Grandma Mary was a child.

The movies show how people dressed then. "I always wore dresses when I was a little girl," Grandma Mary explains. Darla thinks Grandma Mary looked pretty, but Darla likes to wear jeans and T-shirts.

"Like many other women back then, my mother worked at home," Grandma Mary tells Darla. "She took care of our house and my brothers and me."

Today, both men and women work at home. Men and women also have jobs outside the home. Grandma Mary works as a dentist.

Grandma Mary tells Darla about the fun she had as a little girl. Some of the games she played were different from Darla's games. Some were the same.

"Every year, our family went to the Azalea Festival in Wilmington, North Carolina," Grandma Mary says. "People still go to it today."

Every day, people talk and write to share ideas and feelings. This sharing is called **communication**.

Long ago, Grandma Mary wrote letters to her friends and talked to people on the telephone.

Today, she and Darla communicate in the same ways as people did long ago. They also send letters and pictures by e-mail on the computer.

Summary Some things people do have stayed the same. Other things people do have become different.

Review

1 What to Know How are the lives of people today different from the lives of people long ago? How are they the same?

2 Vocabulary What kinds of **communication** did people use long ago to share news?

3 🖍️ **Activity** Ask an older person in your family what life was like when he or she was a child. Share what you learn with your class.

4 ⭐Focus Skill **Sequence** Was Grandma Mary a little girl before or after Darla was born?

Use Visuals

Why It Matters   Looking at pictures helps you understand what you are reading about. Pictures also make what you are reading about more interesting.

Learn

Pictures can tell a story. Sometimes pictures have captions, or words that tell about them. Look at these pictures. Ask questions about what you see.

Family life long ago

Practice

- What are the people doing?

- How are their clothes like your clothes? How are their clothes different?

- How is their home like your home? How is it different?

- What do these pictures tell you about how life has become different?

Apply

As you read this unit, look closely at the pictures to learn what things were like long ago. Think about how pictures help you understand what you read.

Home Tools

A **tool** is something that people use to do work. People have used different kinds of tools in their homes for many years. New technology makes tools better. Look at these tools that people used long ago to see how home tools have changed over time.

DBQ ❶ What do you think it was like to use these tools?

milkman, 1940s

refrigerator, 1930s

potato masher

eggbeater

DBQ ② How are these tools like tools you have at home today?

iron, late 1800s

washer, 1930s

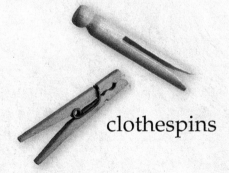
clothespins

sewing machine, late 1800s

DBQ ③ How are these tools different from ones that you use?

typewriter, 1920s

telephone, early 1900s

radio, 1920s

camera, early 1900s

phonograph, late 1800s

television, 1950s

✏ Write About It

How do you think tools have changed over time?

GO ONLINE For more resources, go to www.harcourtschool.com/ss1

💡 **What to Know**
What were schools like long ago?

Vocabulary
change

Sequence

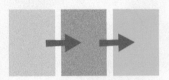

Schools Long Ago

Schools, like other things, change over time. To **change** is to become different.

Long ago, many children learned at home. Others went to schools that had only one room and one teacher. Children of all ages learned together.

One-room school, 1917

170

Today, children go to many kinds of schools. Most schools have many rooms and many teachers. Some ways of learning are the same as in schools long ago. Some ways are different.

Special-needs school

Public school

Home school

We have many tools to help us learn.
In schools long ago, children had tools that
were different from tools we have today.

Long ago, children played many of the same games children play today. They played different games, too. Most of their toys were made by hand.

Look at these two pictures of children playing games long ago. Which game looks like one that is still played today?

Children in History

George S. Parker

George S. Parker was good at thinking up new games. In 1883, when he was only 16 years old, he sold his first game. He and his brothers formed a company. They made many board games that we still play today.

Long ago, some children had to walk miles to get to school. Others rode in wagons. Today, many children ride to school in cars or school buses. Some still walk to school, as children did long ago.

Summary Schools long ago were different from schools today. In some ways, they were the same.

Review

1. **What to Know** What were schools like long ago?

2. **Vocabulary** Name some things that **change** over time.

3. ✏️ **Write** Draw a picture of a school of long ago. Write a sentence to tell about it.

4. ⭐ (Focus Skill) **Sequence** What writing tools did children use before there were pencils and pens like the ones we use today?

175

Put Things in Groups

Why It Matters   You can put things in groups to see how they are the same and how they are different.

Learn

A **table** is a chart that shows things in groups. This table has two groups. One group shows tools of long ago. The other shows tools we use today.

Practice

❶ Which side of the table shows tools children use today?

❷ When did children write on slates? How do you know?

❸ Did children use markers long ago? How does the table show this?

School Tools

Long Ago	Today

Apply

Make It Relevant Make a table. On one side, show tools you would use to make a picture. On the other side, show tools you would use to write a story.

For online activities, go to www.harcourtschool.com/ss1

Communities in the Past

What to Know
What can happen to communities over time?

Vocabulary
past
present
future

 Sequence

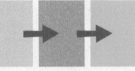

Places grow and change over time just as people do. Marc lives in Elkhart, Indiana. This is what his community looked like in the **past**, or the time before now.

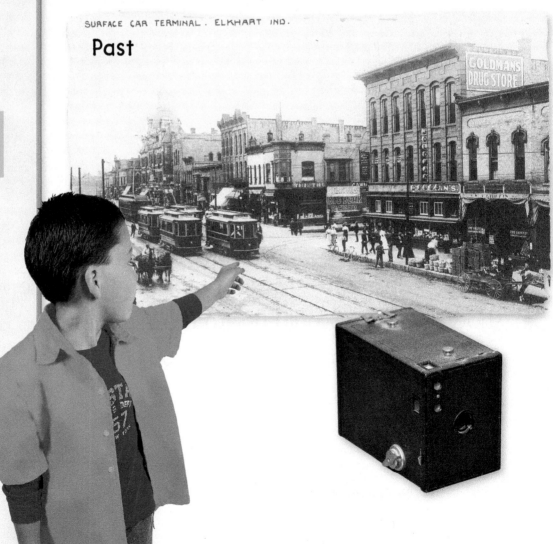

SURFACE CAR TERMINAL. ELKHART IND.

Past

GOLDMANS DRUG STORE

Marc's community has changed a lot. This is what Elkhart looks like in the **present**, or the time now.

Communities change in many ways. People can help change them. Many years ago, families started to move to Elkhart. They built homes, schools, and stores. Elkhart grew bigger.

Present

The kinds of work that people do can change a community, too. Many people came to Elkhart when the first railroad came through the town. Some worked at flour mills and sawmills. Later, many people in Elkhart worked making medicines.

Now people in Elkhart do many different kinds of work. The city is known for making musical instruments. Elkhart will keep changing in the **future**, or the time to come.

Summary Communities change over time. People help change communities.

Review

① **What to Know** What can happen to communities over time?

② **Vocabulary** How was Marc's community different in the **past**?

③ **Activity** Draw a picture to show how your community may have looked in the past.

④ **Sequence** What is Marc's community known for now?

Use a Time Line

Why It Matters   You can show how things change over time.

Learn

A **time line** shows the order in which things have happened. A time line can show days, weeks, months, or years. You read a time line from left to right. The things that happened first are on the left.

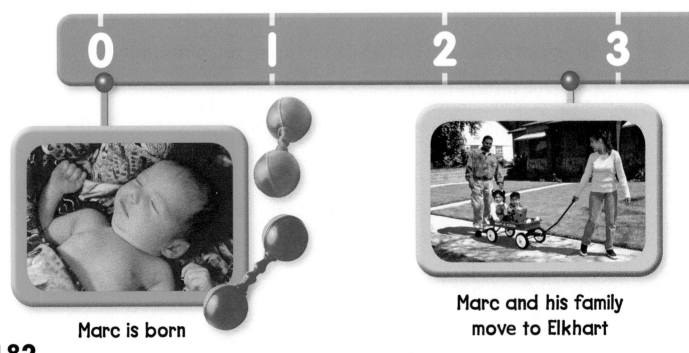

0   1   2   3

Marc is born

Marc and his family move to Elkhart

182

Practice

1 When did Marc start school?

2 What did Marc get when he was six?

3 What happened when Marc was almost three years old?

Apply

Make It Relevant Make a time line to show how you have changed.

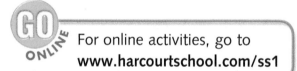

For online activities, go to www.harcourtschool.com/ss1

Marc's first bike

4 5 6 7

Marc starts school

Marc's seventh birthday party

4

Changes in Transportation

In the past, transportation was very slow. It took a long time for people to go places.

Vocabulary
technology

Focus Skill Sequence

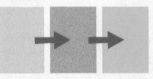

canoe

184

Most people did not take trips to see new places. Many never went far from where they were born.

covered wagon

Fast Fact!

Long ago, mail was carried from the state of Missouri to California by the Pony Express. Riders on horses made the trip in only ten days. That was express—very fast— service then!

People have used technology to make new ways to go places. **Technology** is all of the tools we use to make our lives easier.

Technology has helped transportation in many ways. Boats, trains, cars, planes, and other kinds of transportation are now safer and faster.

Technology is always changing. Today, people can easily go to places that are far away. They can take a trip around the world in just a few days. People have even gone into space. Transportation has changed a lot!

Arrive:Moon

Summary Transportation has changed. Technology has made transportation better now than it was long ago.

Review

1. **What to Know** How has transportation changed over time?

2. **Vocabulary** How has **technology** changed transportation?

3. **Activity** Make a table like the one on page 177 to show transportation long ago and today.

4. **Sequence** Which kind of transportation came first—the airplane, the car, or the canoe?

Tell Fact from Fiction

Why It Matters   Some stories are made up, and some stories are about real things.

Learn

Stories about real things are **nonfiction**. These stories tell only facts. A **fact** is something that is true and not made up.

Stories that are mostly made up are **fiction**. Some stories that are fiction have facts in them to make them seem real.

Sometimes I am up.

Sometimes I am down.

Practice

1. Look at these two books. They both show a kind of transportation.

2. Look at the pictures and the words in each book.

3. Which book is fiction? Which book has only facts?

The Boeing 747 made its first flight in 1969. It carried nearly 500 passengers at speeds of over 500 miles per hour. The 747 can stay in the air for 17 hours and travel more than 8,000 miles. The plane itself is longer than the distance of the Wright Brothers' first flight.

Apply

Make It Relevant Find a book about the past. Do you think it is fiction or nonfiction? How can you tell?

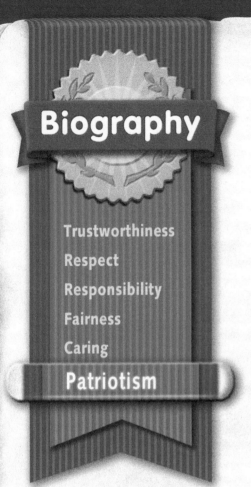

Trustworthiness

Respect

Responsibility

Fairness

Caring

Patriotism

Why Character Counts

✎ How did Neil Armstrong show his patriotism?

Neil Armstrong

When Neil Armstrong was a boy, he liked airplanes and flying. As a teenager, he earned money to pay for flying lessons. Armstrong became a pilot for the United States Navy. In 1962, he joined NASA to learn how to become an astronaut.

Neil Armstrong was the first person to walk on the moon.

Neil Armstrong put an American flag on the moon.

Armstrong first went into space in 1966. Then, in 1969, he became the first person to walk on the moon. As he stepped onto the moon, he said, "That's one small step for man, one giant leap for mankind." Many people on Earth watched his steps. Armstrong put an American flag on the moon.

GO ONLINE For more resources, go to
www.harcourtschool.com/ss1

Time

1930   Present
    Born

1950 Becomes a   1969 Becomes the
pilot for the United   first person to walk
States Navy   on the moon

Find the Changes

Past

194

Present

12:00

195

Review and Test Prep

 The Big Idea

Change In many ways, people today are the same as people who lived long ago. But the way people live has changed over time.

⭐ Sequence

Copy and fill in the chart to show what you learned about how transportation has changed.

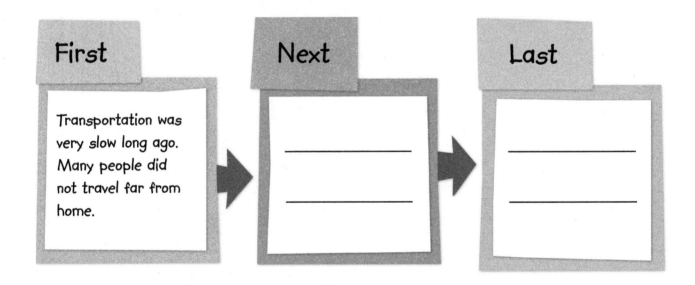

First	Next	Last
Transportation was very slow long ago. Many people did not travel far from home.	_____ _____	_____ _____

✓ Vocabulary

Fill in the blanks with the correct words.

Zack made a __①__ to show the order in which things have happened in his town. He learned how people lived in the __②__, or the time before now. He showed how people live now, in the __③__. Zack learned how things __④__, or become different. One change is that people now use cars instead of horses. Cars are one kind of __⑤__ that makes our lives easier.

Word Bank

change
(p. 170)

past
(p. 178)

present
(p. 179)

time line
(p. 182)

technology
(p. 186)

✓ Facts and Main Ideas

6 How has communication changed over time?

7 How did children get to school long ago?

8 What can change a community?

9 Which of these statements was NOT true long ago?

    A People live in communities.

    B Games are fun.

    C People use e-mail.

    D Children go to school.

10 What has made transportation safer and faster?

    A communication

    B change

    C tools

    D technology

Critical Thinking

11 How might our world change in the future?

12 **Make It Relevant** How has your community changed over time?

Skills

13 Which side of the table shows transportation that we use in the present?

14 Did people fly in big jets in the past? How can you tell?

15 When did people travel on large ships with sails?

16 On which side of the table would you add a space shuttle?

Transportation

Past	Present

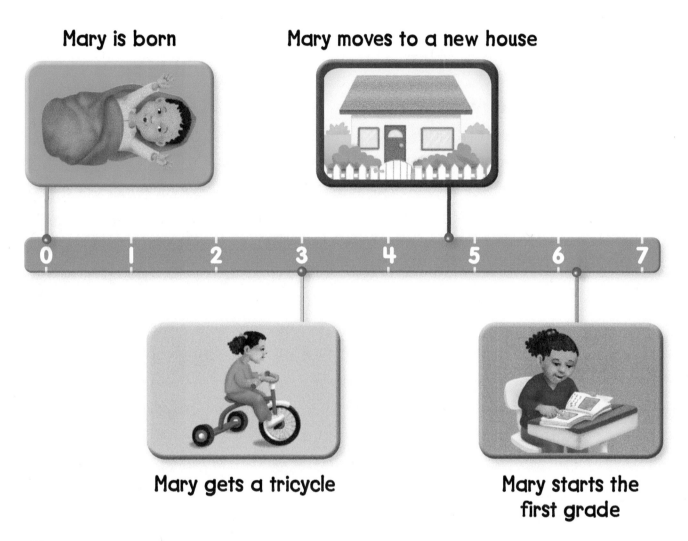

Mary is born

Mary moves to a new house

Mary gets a tricycle

Mary starts the
first grade

17 What does this time line show?

18 When did Mary get a tricycle?

19 What happened when Mary was
almost five?

20 What happened last on this time line?

Unit 4 Activities

Show What You Know

 Unit Writing Activity

Share a Memory All things change. People change, too. Think about when you were younger. What were you like?

Write a Story Write a story about a memory you have from when you were younger.

 Unit Project

Then and Now Scrapbook Make a past and present scrapbook.

- Draw or find pictures of life in the past and now.
- Paste the pictures on pages.
- Share your scrapbook.

Read More

Life Long Ago
by Janine Scott

The Keeping Quilt
by Patricia Polacco

Trains
by Neil Morris

GO ONLINE For more resources, go to
www.harcourtschool.com/ss1

Meeting People

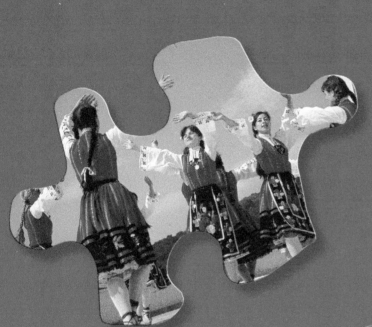

The Big Idea

People

Although Americans may have come from different backgrounds, they share some beliefs.

What to Know

✓ How have Native Americans affected our culture?

✓ How have immigrants added to our culture?

✓ What can folktales tell you about cultures?

✓ How do people celebrate their cultures?

✓ How do families meet their needs?

Unit 5

Meeting People

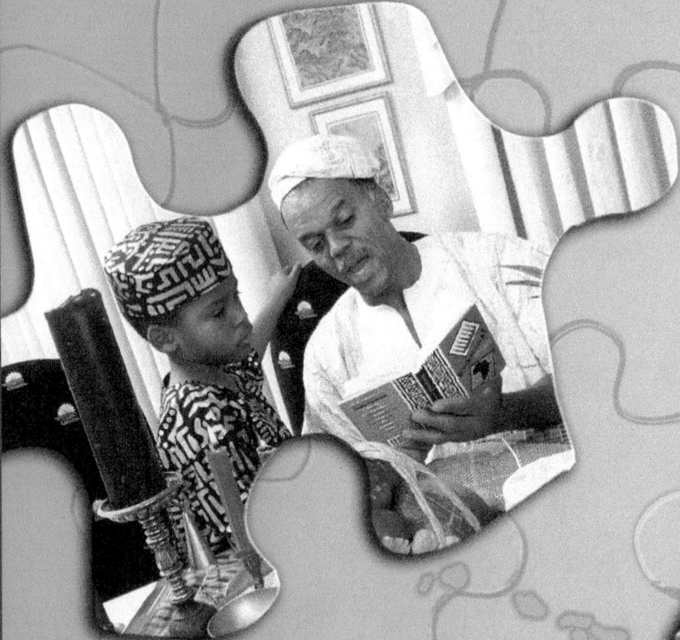

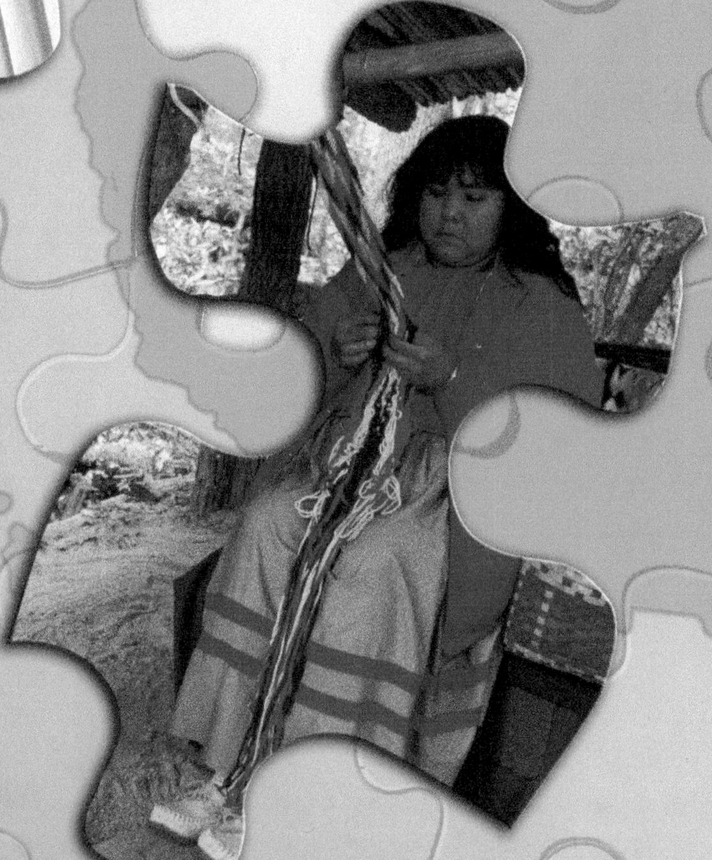

Talk About

People

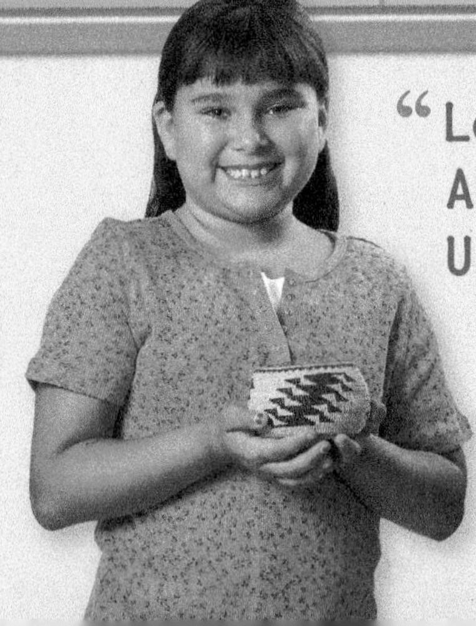

"Long ago, only Native Americans lived in the United States."

"People come from all over the world to live in the United States of America."

"We share our culture in many ways."

Vocabulary

culture A group's way of life.

(page 210)

history The story of what happened in the past. (page 212)

immigrant A person from another part of the world who has come to live in this country. (page 220)

custom A group's way of doing something.

(page 233)

role The part a person plays in a group he or she belongs to. (page 239)

GO ONLINE For more resources, go to www.harcourtschool.com/ss1

Reading Social Studies

Focus Skill

Compare and Contrast

Why It Matters Comparing and contrasting can show you how things are alike and different.

Learn

- You compare two things by thinking about how they are the same.

- You contrast two things by thinking about how they are different.

Read the paragraphs.

Compare
Contrast

Mira and Rosa are best friends. Mira's family is from Poland. She speaks Polish and English. Rosa's family is from Mexico. She speaks Spanish and English.

Mira and Rosa both like to play basketball. They have different favorite foods. Mira likes a Polish soup called chlodnik. Rosa likes tortillas, a Mexican bread.

Practice

Mira

family is from Poland

like a polish soup

She speaks polish

Both

They are best friends.

play basketball

Rosa

family is from Mexico

likes tortillas

She speaks english and spanish

This chart shows how Mira and Rosa are the same and different. What can you add? Copy the chart and fill it in.

Apply

As you read, look for ways to compare and contrast different kinds of people.

How Beetles Became Beautiful

a folktale from Brazil

illustrated by Christopher Corr

Long ago, in the country of Brazil, a brown beetle was crawling toward the Amazon River. Suddenly, a paca ran past her.

"Out of my way, Beetle!" said the plain brown and white rodent. "You are much too slow."

A bright green and yellow parrot had been watching from a tree branch above. "Paca," he called. "What is the problem?"

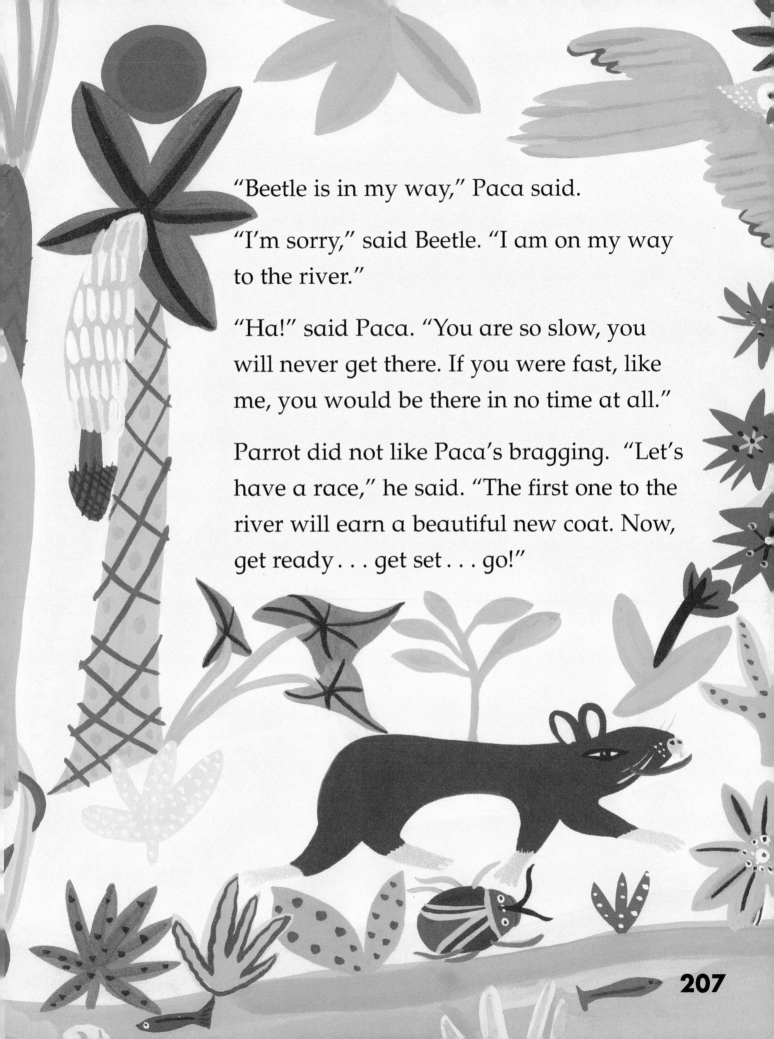

"Beetle is in my way," Paca said.

"I'm sorry," said Beetle. "I am on my way to the river."

"Ha!" said Paca. "You are so slow, you will never get there. If you were fast, like me, you would be there in no time at all."

Parrot did not like Paca's bragging. "Let's have a race," he said. "The first one to the river will earn a beautiful new coat. Now, get ready . . . get set . . . go!"

Paca and Beetle began their race as Parrot flew to the river. Paca ran far ahead of Beetle until he could no longer see her.

"Beetle will never be able to catch up with me," thought Paca. Soon Paca finished the race. "Here I am, Parrot!" he said. "I want my new coat now."

"Look beside you," said Parrot.

Paca looked down and saw Beetle sitting by the river. "How did you get here before me?" he said. "I can run much faster than you can!"

"I did not run," said Beetle. "I flew."

"Oh, no! I forgot Beetle had wings!" said Paca.

"Yes. You were too busy bragging to remember," said Parrot. "Now, Beetle, what colors would you like your coat to be?"

"Green and gold, please," said Beetle.

And so, to this day, beetles are beautiful. Pacas are still plain, but they are a little bit nicer.

Response Corner

1. (Focus Skill) **Compare and Contrast** Who is faster, Paca or Beetle?

2. **Make It Relevant** How is this story like other folktales you know?

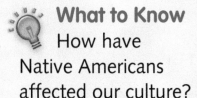
**What to Know**
How have Native Americans affected our culture?

Vocabulary
culture
history
language

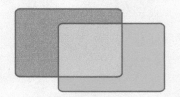**Compare and Contrast**

The First Americans

The first people to live in North America are called Native Americans. There were many different groups, and each group had its own culture.

A **culture** is a group's way of life. Many things, such as food, clothing, and dance, are part of a group's culture.

Nez Perce

The place where each group lived affected its culture. Some Native American groups hunted for their food or caught fish. Others grew food, such as corn and squash.

Navajo

Cherokee

Delaware

These children are listening to a Native American storyteller. He shares the history of his people. **History** is the story of what happened in the past. Some stories in history are myths. A myth is a story about why something in nature is the way it is.

Each Native American group had its own **language**, or way of speaking. Native Americans used language to pass down stories about their culture. We know about their history from these stories, which many Native Americans still tell today.

EST. 1693
Welcome To
HACKENSACK
"A City in Motion"

Early settlers in our country learned a lot from the Native Americans. The Native Americans told them about the land's plants and animals. They showed the settlers how to grow and cook new foods and how to make things they needed.

 What does this map show you about the Native Americans in each place?

Native Americans have a long history in North America. Many groups still live in all parts of the United States. They still follow their cultures.

Hupa Indian basket makers

Summary Native Americans helped our country grow. They shared their cultures with early settlers.

Review

1. **What to Know** How have Native Americans affected our culture?

2. **Vocabulary** How does your family remember its **history**?

3. ✎ **Write** Write two sentences that tell what you have learned about Native American cultures.

4. (Focus Skill) **Compare and Contrast** Look at the Native American crafts on page 214. How are they like things that you use?

215

Follow a Flowchart

Why It Matters   A **flowchart** shows the steps needed to make or do something.

Learn

The title tells what the flowchart is about. Each sentence tells about a step. Arrows show the order of the steps.

Practice

1 What does this flowchart show?

2 What did the Chumash do first?

3 What did they do after they added water to the acorn powder?

Apply

Make It Relevant   Think about something you know how to do, such as brush your teeth. Make a flowchart that tells others how to do it.

How the Chumash Indians Made Acorn Soup

1. Take the shells off the acorns.

2. Crush the acorns into a powder.

3. Add water to the acorn powder.

4. Put hot stones into the soup to cook it.

GO ONLINE

For online activities, go to
www.harcourtschool.com/ss1

Trustworthiness

Respect

Responsibility

Fairness

Caring

Patriotism

Why Character Counts

✎ How did Sacagawea show responsibility?

Sacagawea

Sacagawea was a Native American woman of the Shoshone tribe. As a young woman, Sacagawea met two explorers named Meriwether Lewis and William Clark. This meeting changed her life.

The explorers wanted to travel through the western part of North America. They needed help from a person who knew the land. Sacagawea agreed to be their guide.

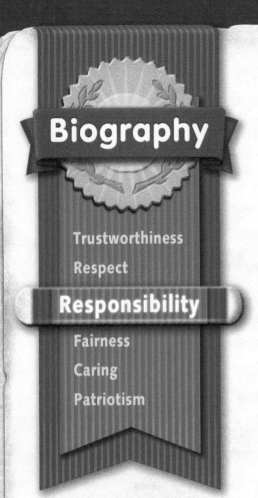

Sacagawea helped Lewis and Clark explore North America.

Sacagawea helped Lewis and Clark speak to Native Americans and learn about the land.

Sacagawea was honored with her picture on a coin.

Sacagawea helped the Native Americans not to be afraid of the explorers. She also got her own tribe to give them horses and food. When Lewis and Clark's important papers fell into the water, Sacagawea saved them. Her responsible acts helped the explorers in many ways.

GO ONLINE For more resources, go to
www.harcourtschool.com/ss1

Time

ca. 1786
Born

ca. 1812
Died

about 1804 Marries
Toussaint Charbonneau

1805 Joins explorers
Lewis and Clark as
their guide

219

 What to Know
How have immigrants added to our culture?

Vocabulary

immigrant
world

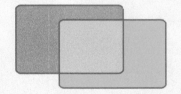 **Compare and Contrast**

People Find New Homes

Anahat, Kweli, Juan, and Yana are making a scrapbook about their families. They are all immigrants to the United States. An **immigrant** is a person from another part of the world who has come to live in this country. The **world** is all the people and places on Earth.

Anahat is from India.

Kweli is from Kenya.

Juan is from El Salvador.

Yana is from Russia.

221

Families who come to the United States bring their cultures with them. They share their cultures with others. Many kinds of food, clothing, and recreation have been brought to this country by immigrants.

Anahat's family owns an Indian restaurant.

Kweli's family sells African art.

People of different cultures live and work together in their community. Learning about one another and sharing cultures help us get along.

Yana's mother teaches ballet, which she learned in Russia.

Juan's grandmother sells cloth that she learned to make in El Salvador.

People have come to the United States from other places for many years. Some immigrants have crossed the ocean from countries such as Ireland, Italy, and China. Others have come by land from Canada and Mexico.

Ellis Island

Russian passport

People are still coming to the United States today. When people move here, they can keep their cultures. They can share in American culture, too.

Summary Immigrants move to the United States from all over the world. The cultures they bring help our country change and grow.

Review

1. **What to Know** How have immigrants added to our culture?

2. **Vocabulary** What is the **world**?

3. **Activity** What countries did people in your family live in before they came to the United States? Mark the places on a globe or a map.

4. **Compare and Contrast** How are Anahat, Kweli, Juan, and Yana like you? How are they different?

225

Points of View

The Sidewalk Reporter asks:

"What do you like about having many cultures in your community?"

David

"I can taste foods from around the world in the restaurants in my community."

Mr. Fernandez

"We like learning about other cultures at festivals in our community."

View from the Past

Robert C. Weaver: Many Cultures

The United States made a law saying that people of every culture have the right to live in any community. Robert C. Weaver's job was to make sure people followed this new law.

Mr. Peters

"I am learning some French words from the woman who owns the French bakery in my neighborhood."

Mrs. Martinez

"Artists from different cultures make murals for people in the community to enjoy."

Kelsey

"I love watching street performers play their special kinds of music!"

It's Your Turn

- What cultures do you have in your community?
- How do different cultures make your community interesting?

227

What to Know
What can folktales tell you about cultures?

Vocabulary
folktale
religion

Compare and Contrast

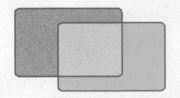

Expressing Culture

Every culture has folktales. A **folktale** is a story passed from person to person. Folktales can tell about a culture's people, the places where they live, and their beliefs.

Folktales can tell about nature.

THE NAME OF THE TREE

A BANTU FOLKTALE RETOLD BY Celia Barker Lottridge
ILLUSTRATED BY Ian Wallace

Folktales can teach lessons and help you learn what people believe. Folktales can also show that cultures have different religions. A **religion** is a belief in a god or gods.

Folktales can teach lessons.

Folktales can tell about beliefs.

Words, pictures, dance, and other arts are all used to tell these stories. Most folktales were told for many, many years before they were written down on paper.

Vietnamese story cloth

Mexican puppets

Hawaiian dancers

Summary People share their cultures through folktales. Folktales can tell about the beliefs of a culture.

Review

1. **What to Know** What can folktales tell you about cultures?

2. **Vocabulary** What is a **religion**?

3. **Activity** Act out a folktale that tells about a culture that is different from your own.

4. **Compare and Contrast** Read or listen to two stories from different cultures. How are they the same? How are they different?

Sharing Celebrations

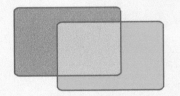
In Li's culture, the celebration of Chinese New Year lasts for 15 days. A **celebration** is a time to be happy about something special.

Each day of Chinese New Year has a different **custom**, or way of doing something. It is a custom to celebrate the last night of Chinese New Year with a Lantern Festival.

Li did not grow up in China. He is learning about his Chinese culture from the celebrations and customs of his family and his community.

Anita's family is from Mexico. Every year on May 5, they celebrate Cinco de Mayo. Cinco de Mayo is a celebration to honor Mexico.

There are many kinds of celebrations in our country. Each culture is proud of its customs. Sharing special celebrations helps us learn about each other.

Children all over the world share birthday celebrations with friends and family.

Summary People celebrate special times. We share our culture's customs when we celebrate with others.

Review

① **What to Know** How do people celebrate their cultures?

② **Vocabulary** What is one **celebration** that you share with your family?

③ 🖌 **Activity** Make a collage about cultures. Show different customs and celebrations.

④ ⭐Focus Skill **Compare and Contrast** How are Chinese New Year and American New Year celebrations the same? How are they different?

Follow a Route

Why It Matters   A **route** on a map shows how to get from one place to another.

Learn

In many communities, people share their cultures through parades. This map shows a parade route in a community.

Practice

① How is the parade route shown?

② In which direction will the parade go on First Avenue?

③ What will the parade pass on Rose Street?

④ Where does the parade route start and end?

Apply

Make It Relevant   Make a map of your community. Show the route you follow home from school.

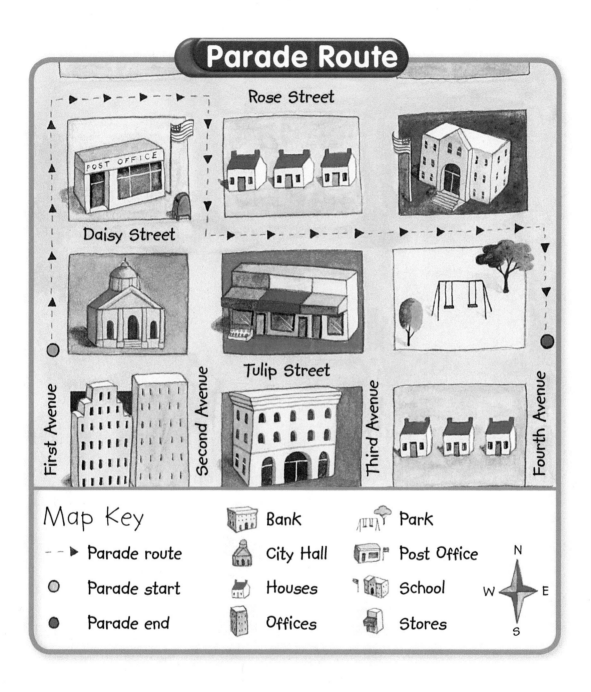

Parade Route

Rose Street

Daisy Street

Tulip Street

First Avenue

Second Avenue

Third Avenue

Fourth Avenue

Map Key

- ▶ Parade route
- ○ Parade start
- ● Parade end
- Bank
- City Hall
- Houses
- Offices
- Park
- Post Office
- School
- Stores

N
W E
S

Map and Globe Skills

GO ONLINE
For online activities, go to
www.harcourtschool.com/ss1

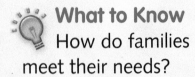 **What to Know**
How do families
meet their needs?

Vocabulary
role

 **Compare
and Contrast**

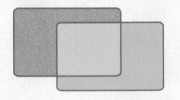

Families Around the World

People around the world are
alike in many ways. They belong to
groups such as their family, school,
and community.

Each person in a family has a role. A **role** is the part that a person plays in a group he or she belongs to. Family members help take care of each other.

South Africa

Japan

239

Families all over the world have the same needs for food, clothing, and shelter. Some families meet their needs in the same ways your family does. Some meet their needs in different ways.

Mongolia

Algeria

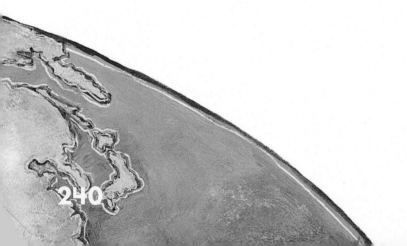

Summary Families all over the world meet their needs in different ways.

Review

❶ **What to Know** How do families meet their needs?

❷ **Vocabulary** What is a **role**?

❸ ✎ **Write** Write sentences about your roles in your family, school, and community.

❹ (Focus Skill) **Compare and Contrast** Look at the families in this lesson. How are they like your family? How are they different?

How  Got Thin: A Native American Folktale

 Coyote   Evening Star

One night, fat saw a bright light go across the sky. It was beautiful . wanted to ride on .

Every night, asked for a ride.

Every night, said, "No, I go too fast."

One night, got tired of hearing .

"Get on my back," told him.

 climbed on. went very fast. could not hold on.

He fell to . He hit so hard that he got as flat as a . That is how got thin.

242

Word Match

Match each picture with the correct word.

history

celebration

folktale

world

Review and Test Prep

 **The Big Idea**

People Although Americans may have come from different backgrounds, they share some beliefs.

Focus Skill Compare and Contrast

Copy and fill in the chart to compare and contrast Native Americans and immigrants.

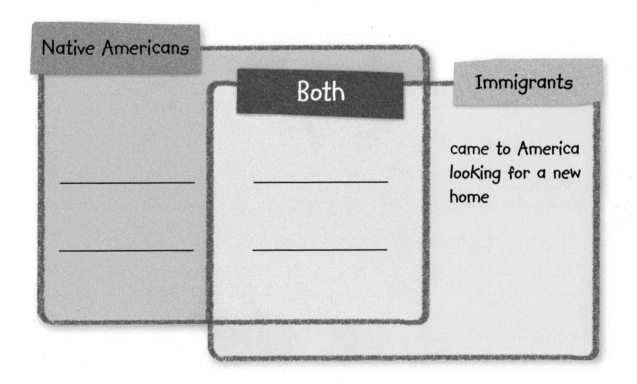

Native Americans

Both

Immigrants

came to America looking for a new home

Vocabulary

Give another example to explain each word.

Words	Examples	
❶ culture (p. 210)	Native Americans' way of life	
❷ history (p. 212)	Americans fought a war for freedom	
❸ immigrant (p. 220)	a person who moves to America from Germany	
❹ custom (p. 233)	Chinese dragon dance	
❺ role (p. 239)	pitcher for softball team	

Facts and Main Ideas

❻ Who were the first people in North America?

❼ Where do immigrants come from?

❽ What is a folktale?

❾ Which culture celebrates the New Year for 15 days?

    A German   **C** Mexican

    B Chinese   **D** American

❿ Which is NOT a need that families have?

    A food   **C** clothing

    B shelter   **D** bicycles

Critical Thinking

⓫ How are immigrants today like the first settlers? How are they different?

⓬ **Make It Relevant** How does your family celebrate your culture?

Skills

How to Make a Chinese Lantern

❶ Fold a piece of paper in half. Make small cuts along the fold.

❷ Unfold the paper. Paste the short edges together.

❸ Paste a strip of paper across one end to make a handle.

⓭ What does this flowchart show?

⓮ How many steps are in the flowchart?

⓯ What is the first step?

⓰ What is the last step?

246

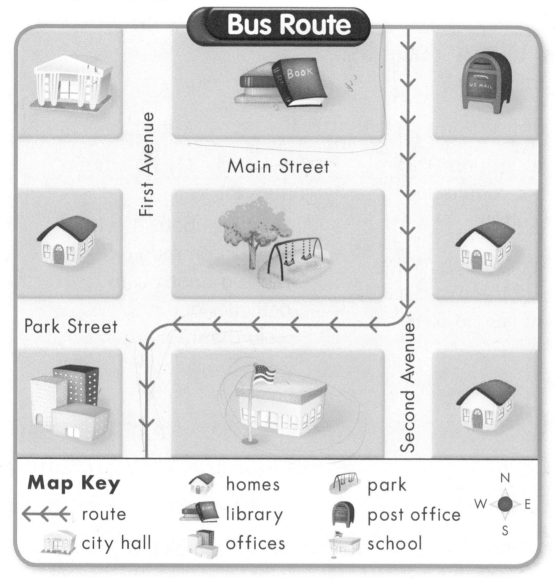

Bus Route

First Avenue

Main Street

Book

Park Street

Second Avenue

Map Key

← ← route

🏠 homes

🏛 park

📚 library

📮 post office

🏢 city hall

🏢 offices

🏫 school

N W E S

⑰ Could you take this bus to get from city hall to the school?

⑱ In which direction does the route go on Park Street?

⑲ What will the route pass on First Avenue?

⑳ Could you take this bus to get from the library to the offices?

Show What You Know

 Unit Writing Activity

Compare Cultures Think about your culture and another culture.

Write a Paragraph Write about how the two cultures are the same and different.

 Unit Project

Culture Fair Plan a school culture fair.

- Find out about a culture in your community.
- Make a booth with activities and displays.
- Hold the fair.

Read More

HarperCollins

Families
by Ann Morris

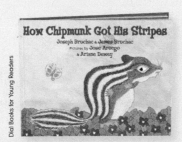

Dial Books for Young Readers

How Chipmunk Got His Stripes
by Joseph Bruchac

Herald Press

Henner's Lydia
by Marguerite De Angeli

GO ONLINE For more resources, go to
www.harcourtschool.com/ss1

The Marketplace

The Big Idea

Markets

People trade goods and services with each other. They make choices about how to spend their money.

What to Know

✔ Why are goods and services important?

✔ What kinds of jobs do people do?

✔ Why do people buy and sell?

✔ How are goods made in a factory?

The Marketplace

" You can trade money for goods and services you want to buy. "

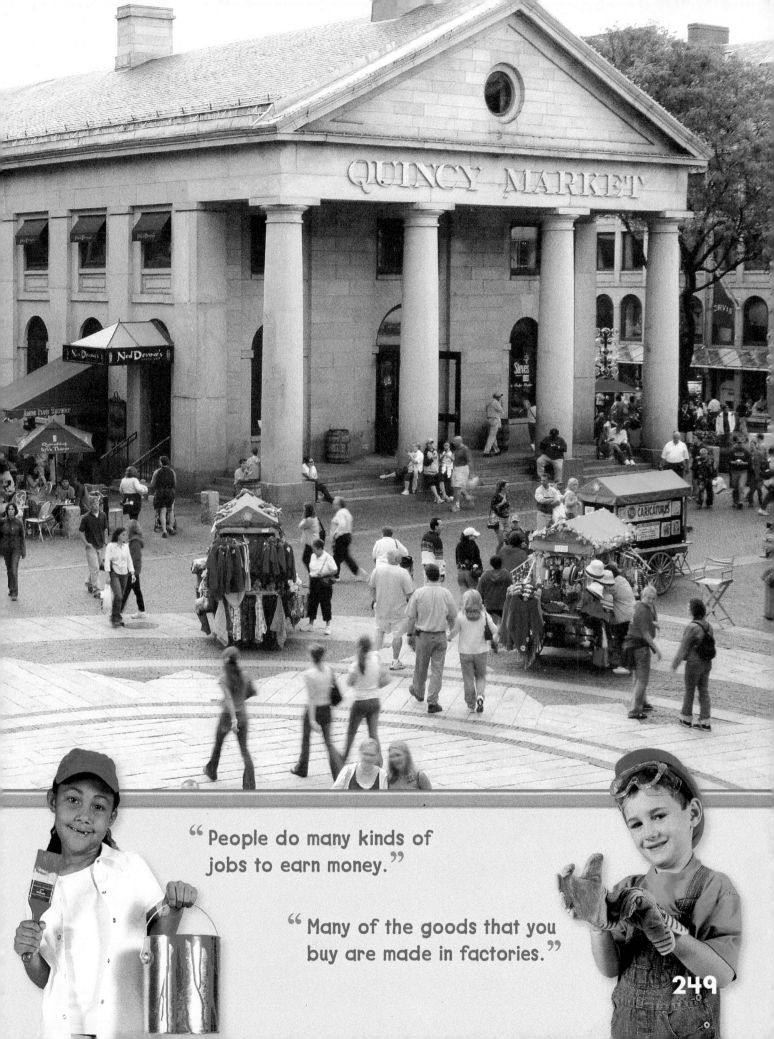

QUINCY MARKET

"People do many kinds of jobs to earn money."

"Many of the goods that you buy are made in factories."

Vocabulary

goods Things that people make or grow to sell.

(page 260)

services Kinds of work people do for others for money.

(page 262)

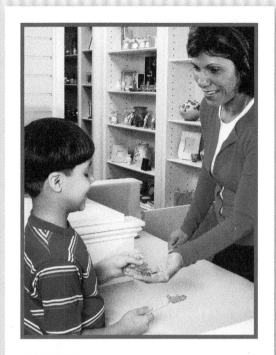

trade To give one thing to get another thing. (page 282)

market A place where people buy and sell goods. (page 280)

factory A building in which people use machines to make goods. (page 290)

GO **ONLINE** For more resources, go to www.harcourtschool.com/ss1

Reading Social Studies

Focus Skill Recall and Retell

Why It Matters Recalling and retelling can help you put information in your own words.

Learn

- To recall is to remember.

- To retell is to tell about something in your own words.

Read the paragraphs.

Recall Mr. Carson goes to work every morning and is gone all day. He put this ad in his city's newspaper.

WANTED: Person to do work around the house from Monday to Friday. Must love dogs.

Practice

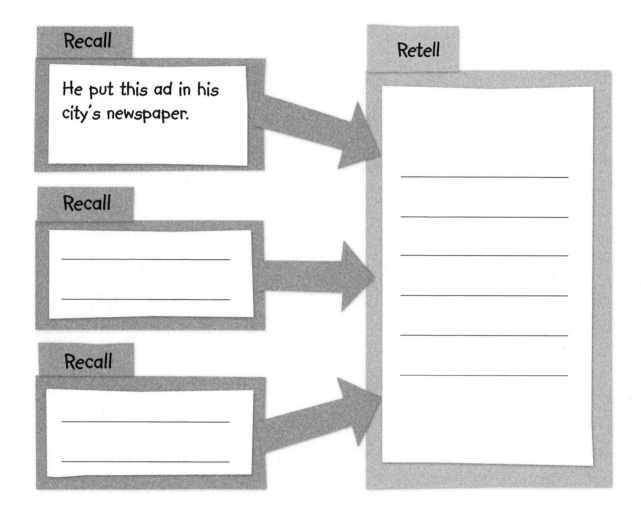

Recall

He put this ad in his city's newspaper.

Recall

_____

_____

Recall

_____

_____

Retell

_____

_____

_____

_____

_____

_____

_____

Use this chart to write details you recall from what you just read. Then retell what you read in your own words. Copy the chart and fill it in.

Apply

As you read, stop to recall and retell what you have read.

ONE AFTERNOON

by Yumi Heo

Minho liked to do errands with his mother.
One afternoon, they went to
the Laundromat to drop off their clothes
and then to the beauty salon
to get his mother's hair cut.

254

At the ice cream store,
Minho got a vanilla cone.
They looked in the pet store window
at the puppies, kittens, hamsters,
and birds.

255

They picked up his father's shoes at the shoe repair store and got food for dinner at the supermarket.

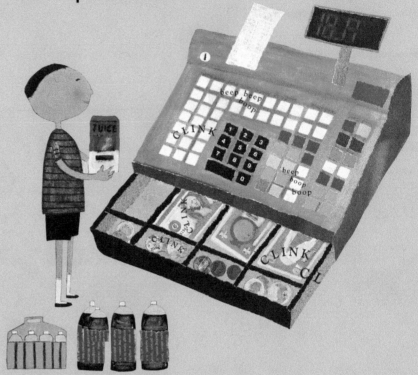

Last of all, Minho and his mother went back to the Laundromat to get the clothes they had dropped off.

Traffic was very heavy on the street
because of the construction.
A fire engine tried to get through.
The El train was passing by above.

Near Minho's apartment,
children were playing stickball.
Minho and his mother were very
happy to get back in their quiet home.

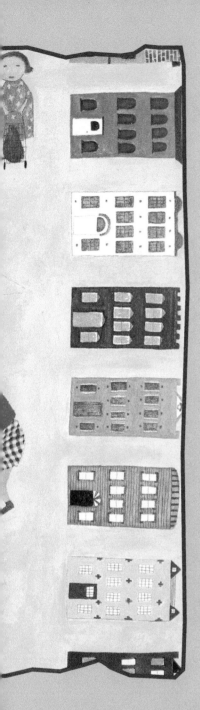

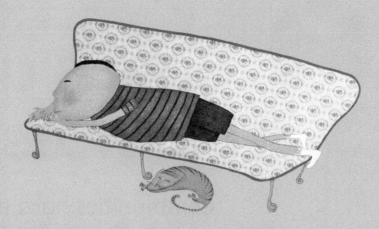

Minho was tired and fell asleep on the couch. But from the bathroom . . . PLUNK!

Response Corner

1. (Focus Skill) **Recall and Retell** What services did Minho and his mother use?

2. **Make It Relevant** Write about the kinds of goods and services your family uses in your community.

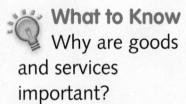
What to Know
Why are goods and services important?

Vocabulary

goods
services
money

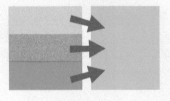
Recall and Retell

Goods and Services

Communities have many kinds of workers. Some workers make goods. **Goods** are things that people make or grow to sell.

Some workers sell goods. People can buy goods in stores. Communities have many kinds of stores that sell many kinds of goods.

Some workers sell services. **Services** are kinds of work people do for others for money. **Money** is what people use to pay for goods and services. You use many kinds of services in your community.

Mail carrier

Hair stylist

Services and Prices

Haircut..........................$10

Shampoo and cut.................$12

Shampoo, cut, and style.......$16

Veterinarian

Bus driver

Summary Many people work selling goods or services. People use money to buy goods and services.

Review

1. **What to Know** Why are goods and services important?

2. **Vocabulary** What is **money**?

3. ✏️ **Write** Write a sentence about a time when you used a service.

4. ⭐(Focus Skill) **Recall and Retell** Where can people buy goods?

Read a Picture Graph

Why It Matters   A **picture graph** uses pictures to show how many there are of something.

Learn

The title of a picture graph tells you what it is about. The key tells you what each picture stands for.

Look at each row from left to right. Count to see how many baskets of each kind of apple were sold.

Practice

1 Of which kind of apple were the most baskets sold?

2 Were more baskets of red apples or yellow apples sold?

3 Of which kind of apple were the fewest baskets sold?

Baskets of Apples Sold

Green Apples	🍏 🍏 🍏 🍏 🍏 🍏 🍏
Red Apples	🍎 🍎 🍎
Yellow Apples	🍎 🍎 🍎 🍎 🍎

Key
🍎 = one basket

Apply

Make It Relevant   Make a picture graph. Show how many children in your class like each kind of apple.

GO ONLINE For online activities, go to
www.harcourtschool.com/ss1

Points of View

The Sidewalk Reporter asks:
"What goods and services are important to your family?"

Ms. Clark

"Fruits and vegetables are important goods. Eating them keeps my family healthy."

Louis

"Bus drivers do an important service. They help people get to work and to school on time."

View from the Past

Rosie the Riveter

"Rosie the Riveter" was the name of a woman on a poster used in World War II. She stood for all the women who worked to help the United States in the war.

Megan

"Books are important goods. They help me learn new things."

Mr. Winslow

"Builders do an important service. They build homes for people to live in."

James

"Sanitation workers do an important service. They take garbage away from our homes and put it in a safe place."

We Can Do It!

It's Your Turn

- What kinds of goods are important to you?
- What work would you like to do some day?

Jobs People Do

What to Know
What kinds of jobs do people do?

Vocabulary
job
business
volunteer

Recall and Retell

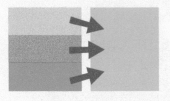

Mrs. Brown has a job in her community. A **job** is work that a person does to earn money. Mrs. Brown also does her job because she likes it.

Mrs. Brown owns a business. In a **business**, people sell goods or services. Mrs. Brown's business sells a service. The business helps people find jobs.

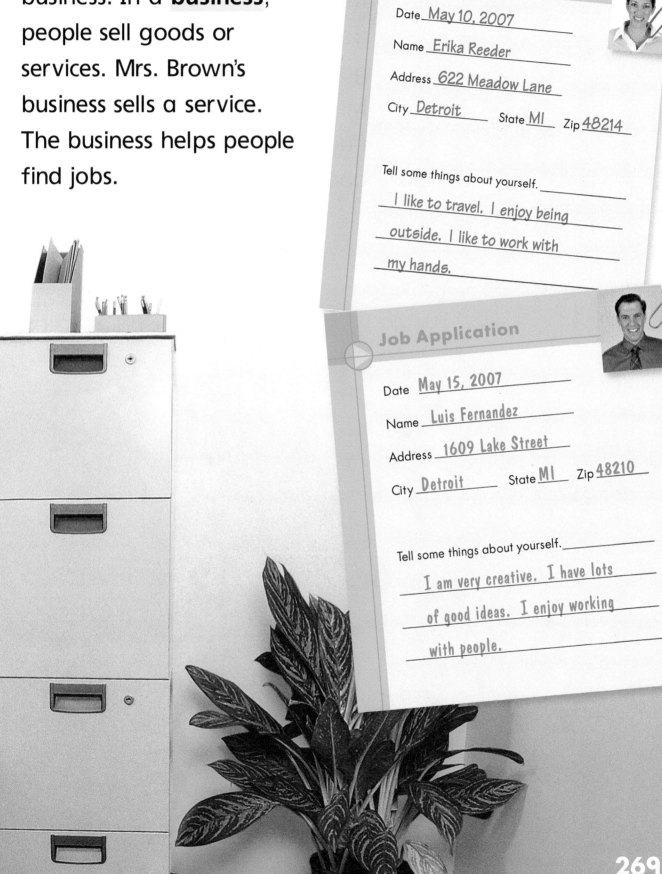

Job Application

Date May 10, 2007

Name Erika Reeder

Address 622 Meadow Lane

City Detroit   State MI   Zip 48214

Tell some things about yourself.
I like to travel. I enjoy being outside. I like to work with my hands.

Job Application

Date May 15, 2007

Name Luis Fernandez

Address 1609 Lake Street

City Detroit   State MI   Zip 48210

Tell some things about yourself.
I am very creative. I have lots of good ideas. I enjoy working with people.

Purchase Order

Number of Boxes Ordered	Number of Boxes Received	Cost per Box
200	200	$3.00

	Total Items	200
	Cost per Item	$3.00
	Total Cost	$600.00

Delivered by: _Erika Reeder_

There are many kinds of jobs. Many people have jobs making goods. Others have jobs taking goods where they need to go. Mrs. Brown helped Ms. Reeder find a job driving a truck to take goods to stores.

TRANSport

Many people work at jobs that help sell goods. Mrs. Brown found Mr. Fernandez a job making up ads. His ads tell people why they should buy certain goods.

Farm Fresh Indiana Eggs

Children in History

Addie Laird

Addie Laird was a young girl who worked in a factory. Long ago, many children had jobs in factories. They worked very hard all day, and the factory machines were not safe. When people saw this picture of Addie, they wanted to change the law. Now a child's job is to learn in school.

Some people work at taking care of their home and the people who live in it. Many people also do work for others at home. Mr. Parker gives piano lessons. Mrs. Brown takes her daughter to his house.

On Saturday, Mrs. Brown takes food to people who need it. On that day, she is a volunteer. A **volunteer** works without pay to help people.

Summary There are many kinds of jobs people can do to earn money. People can also volunteer to help others.

Review

1. **What to Know** What kinds of jobs do people do?

2. **Vocabulary** What kind of **business** would you like to own?

3. **Activity** Dress up to act out a job you would like to do.

4. **Recall and Retell** What does Mrs. Brown do to earn money?

Preview and Question

Why It Matters   New ideas are easier to understand when you write what you have learned. A K-W-L chart helps you write down important facts before and after you read.

Learn

The K-W-L chart below shows some information about working. Copy the chart.

● What do you already know about working?

● What do you want to know about working?

K-W-L Chart

What I Know	What I Want to Know	What I Learned
People work to earn money.	Where do people work?	

Practice

Read the paragraph. Write a new fact you learned.

Where a person works depends on the kind of job he or she has. People work in offices, stores, restaurants, and other places. Some people work on farms. Some work in hospitals. Others make goods or do services at home.

Apply

Make a K-W-L chart about buyers and sellers. As you read the next lesson, fill in the chart.

Trustworthiness
Respect
Responsibility
Fairness
Caring
Patriotism

Cesar Chavez

Cesar Chavez knew about the life of a farmworker. When he was a child, he and his family had to give up their farm in Arizona. They had to travel all the time to work in other people's fields. The work was hard, the hours were long, and the pay was low. Workers were treated badly. Cesar Chavez saw that this was not fair.

Why Character Counts

✏ How did Cesar Chavez help farmworkers get fair treatment?

Cesar Chavez started a group that is now called the United Farm Workers of America to help workers.

Cesar Chavez talked to people everywhere about farmworkers' rights.

In 1962, Cesar Chavez formed a union, or a group of many workers. The union held a strike. In a strike, people will not work until they are treated fairly. The farmworkers wanted better pay and health care. Cesar Chavez spent his life working to make sure people were treated fairly.

GO ONLINE For more resources, go to www.harcourtschool.com/ss1

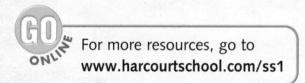

Time

1927
Born

1993
Died

1962 Starts a union for farmworkers

1992 The United Farm Workers Union wins better pay for workers

Helping Others

Volunteers work without pay to help people. Children can be volunteers, too. They can join a group that does projects to help people.

Citymeals-on-Wheels is a group in New York City that helps older citizens. This group delivers food and other items to the elderly. Every year, schoolchildren all over the city volunteer with this group.

Children make holiday cards for older citizens. They draw a picture and write a holiday message on each card. Then, the cards are taken to older citizens' homes.

In one year, New York's children made more than 20,000 cards! Older citizens enjoy getting handmade cards from the children.

There are many other groups in which children can volunteer. Some of these groups are Kids Care Clubs, America Youth Service, and Youth Volunteer Corps of America.

Holiday cards are taken to older citizens' homes.

Make It Relevant How could you help older citizens in your community?

 What to Know
Why do people buy and sell?

Vocabulary
market
trade
save

 **Recall and Retell**

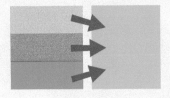

Buyers and Sellers

Amy's community has a large outdoor market. A **market** is a place where people buy and sell goods.

Refreshments

Bonsai Booth

Amy has money to spend at the market. She is going to buy a gift for her grandmother. Amy sees that there are many choices. She will think about what gift her grandmother would like best. Amy will also think about how much she has to spend.

Buyers trade with sellers to get the goods and services they want. When people **trade**, they give one thing to get another thing. Amy will trade some of her money to get a gift for her grandmother.

How Money Moves

Money moves from person to person as people buy and sell goods and services.

1. Amy earns money selling lemonade.

2. Amy buys a gift from Mr. Lopez.

3. Mr. Lopez pays Mr. Harris for fixing his car.

4. Mr. Harris buys lemonade.

Amy does not spend all of her money at once. She spends some of it, but she saves some, too. To **save** means to keep some money to use later. Most people put their money in a bank. A bank is a business that keeps money safe.

" A penny saved
is a penny earned. "

—Benjamin Franklin

Summary Buyers trade money with sellers for goods and services. People save some money to use later.

Review

1. **What to Know** Why do people buy and sell?

2. **Vocabulary** What do people do at a **market**?

3. ✎ **Write** Make a shopping list. Tell where you would go to buy the goods on your list.

4. (Focus Skill) **Recall and Retell** How is Amy both a seller and a buyer?

285

Make a Choice When Buying

Why It Matters   Some things are scarce. When something is **scarce**, there is not enough of it to meet everyone's wants. **Wants** are things people would like to have. People cannot buy everything they want. They must make choices.

Learn

When you make a choice, you give up some things to get other things you want. Follow these steps to make a good choice.

❶ Ask yourself if you want this thing more than other things.

❷ Think about what you would give up to have this thing.

❸ Make your choice.

Practice

1. Look at the pictures. Think about which thing you would like to buy.

2. Follow the steps for making a choice.

3. Tell what choice you would make and why.

Apply

Make It Relevant   Think about two things you would like to have. Tell how you could make a choice between the two things.

Field Trip

Read About

The Royal Oak Farmers Market was started in 1925 just outside of Detroit, Michigan. Today, many people come to this market to buy locally grown fruits and vegetables. People also come for the flea market that is held there every Sunday.

Find

United States

Royal Oak, Michigan

Royal Oak Farmers Market

Buyers can choose from many fruits and vegetables sold at the farmers market.

Some people come to the market to buy plants or flowers.

At the flea market, buyers can find furniture, jewelry, and many other items.

During the fall, families search for the perfect pumpkin.

ROYAL OAK FARMERS MARKET
Everything from the Farm, Garden, Greenhouse and Orchard

A Virtual Tour

GO ONLINE For more resources, go to www.harcourtschool.com/ss1

4

Working in a Factory

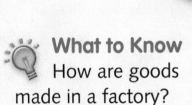
We use crayons in school and at home to make pictures. Did you ever wonder how crayons are made?

Crayons are made in a factory. A **factory** is a building in which people use machines to make goods.

Manufacturing

290

Many people work at the crayon factory. Different workers do different jobs. Some people work in offices to take orders or to run the factory. Others work together to make the crayons, pack them, and send them to stores. Then workers at the stores sell the crayons.

Packaging

Transporting

How Crayons Are Made

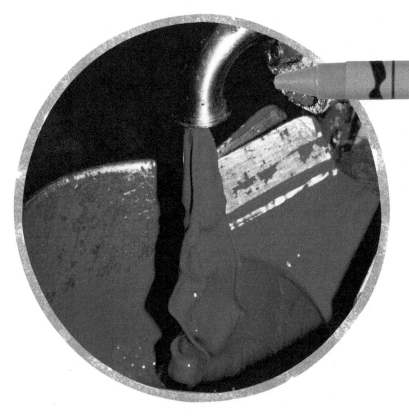

Step 1

First, the factory workers mix hot, melted wax and colorings. The wax will give the crayons their shape. The colorings will give them their colors.

Step 2

Next, workers pour the hot colored wax into molds to shape the crayons.

Step 3

Then, the molds are cooled with water so that the crayons get hard.

Step 4

Workers look at the crayons after they come out of the molds. These workers make sure that the crayons look right.

Step 5

In another part of
the factory, workers
use machines to
make labels and paste
them on the crayons.

Step 6

More workers put
the crayons in boxes
of different sizes. The
boxes are then packed
and taken to stores.

The crayons go to places around the
world. Your crayons went from the factory
to a store and then to your school.

294

Fast Fact!

Each crayon has a label that tells what color it is. These labels are in 12 different languages. Why do you think the labels are in so many languages?

azul

grün

rouge

きいろ

Summary A factory is a building in which many people use machines to make goods. People in a factory have different jobs.

Review

1 **What to Know** How are goods made in a factory?

2 **Vocabulary** How is a **factory** different from a market?

3 **Activity** Draw an idea for a machine that makes something you use in the classroom. Label the parts.

4 **Recall and Retell** How do crayons get their shape?

Use a Bar Graph

Why It Matters   A **bar graph** uses bars to show how many or how much. You can use a bar graph to compare numbers or amounts of things.

Learn

The title of a graph tells you what it shows. This graph shows how many boxes of crayons were sold at different stores.

Read each row from left to right. Count the blocks to learn how many boxes were sold at each store.

Practice

1 How many boxes did Mrs. Garcia's store sell?

2 Whose store sold the most boxes?

3 Who sold more boxes—Ms. Lee or Mr. Smith?

Boxes of Crayons Sold

	0	1	2	3	4	5	6	7	8
Mrs. Garcia's Store									
Mr. King's Store									
Ms. Lee's Store									
Mr. Smith's Store									

Apply

Make It Relevant Make a bar graph to show how many children in your class like each color crayon.

For online activities, go to www.harcourtschool.com/ss1

Chart and Graph Skills

You're in BUSINESS

YOU'RE IN BUSINESS

MAKE A SIGN

Lemonade 25¢

MESS GO BACK 2 SPACES

Get PITCHER

RETURN HOME

TRADE MONEY FOR GOODS

Get CUPS MOVE AHEAD 2 SPACES

SUGAR

MARKET

LOOK AROUND THE MARKET

Forgot MONEY GO BACK 2 SPACES

GO TO MARKET

GET BAG

Forgot Lemons GO BACK 1 SPACE

GET lemons

START

298

Play a game.

You will need:

- 1 or 2 players
- a spinner
- a coin or counter

Spin the spinner, and play until your lemonade stand is open. For two players, take turns and race to the finish.

Online Adventures GO ONLINE

Eco is shopping for a picnic. Visit the online market together to buy supplies. Play now, at www.harcourtschool.com/ss1

Review and Test Prep

The Big Idea

Markets People trade goods and services with each other. They make choices about how to spend their money.

(Focus Skill) Recall and Retell

Recall important ideas from this unit. Write them in the Recall boxes of the chart. Then retell what you remember about the ideas.

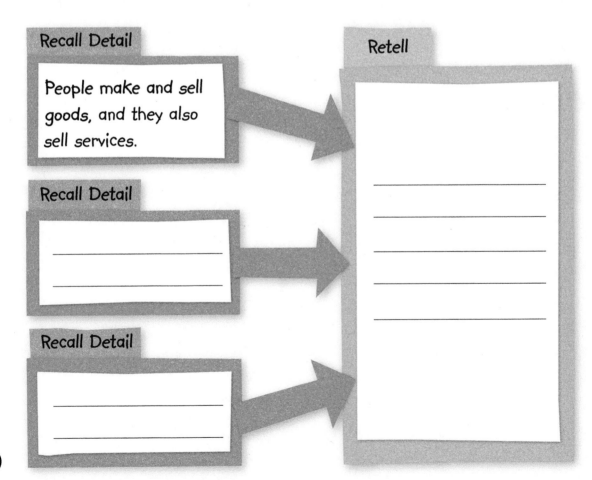

Recall Detail

People make and sell goods, and they also sell services.

Recall Detail

Recall Detail

Retell

Vocabulary

Write the word that goes with each meaning.

1 a place where people buy and sell goods

2 a building in which people use machines to make goods

3 things people make or grow to sell

4 work people do for others for money

5 to give one thing to get another

Word Bank

goods
(p. 260)

services
(p. 262)

market
(p. 280)

trade
(p. 282)

factory
(p. 290)

Facts and Main Ideas

6 Where do people buy goods in a community?

7 What do people use to pay for goods and services?

8 Why do people work at a job?

9 Which of these is a good?

    A haircut   **C** car wash

    B doctor   **D** bicycle

10 Which of these is a place where people put their money to keep it safe?

    A bank   **C** factory

    B market   **D** business

⑪ Why do people save money?

⑫ **Make It Relevant** How do volunteers help people in your community?

Skills

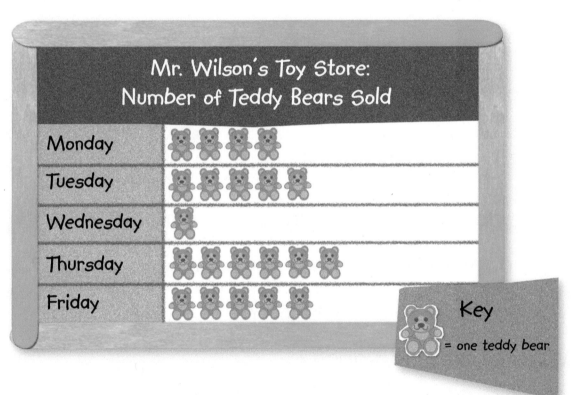

Mr. Wilson's Toy Store:
Number of Teddy Bears Sold

Monday	🧸🧸🧸🧸
Tuesday	🧸🧸🧸🧸🧸
Wednesday	🧸
Thursday	🧸🧸🧸🧸🧸🧸
Friday	🧸🧸🧸🧸🧸

Key
🧸 = one teddy bear

⑬ What does this graph show?

⑭ How many teddy bears were sold on Monday?

⑮ On which two days were the same number of teddy bears sold?

⑯ On which day were the fewest teddy bears sold?

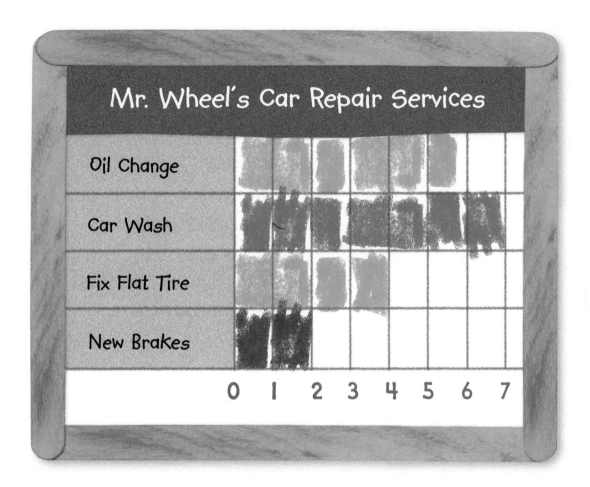

⑰ What services does Mr. Wheel do for people?

⑱ What service did the most people need?

⑲ How many people took their cars to Mr. Wheel for an oil change?

⑳ How many people needed new brakes?

Unit 6 Activities

Show What You Know

 Unit Writing Activity

Money Think about how you use your money.

Write a Story Make up a story about someone choosing how to use his or her money.

 Unit Project

Classroom Market Make a class market.

- Choose what you will sell.
- Draw goods or services and money.
- Sell the goods or services so you can buy more.

Read More

Jobs Around My Neighborhood
by Gladys Rosa-Mendoza

Trees to Paper
by Inez Snyder

Grandpa's Corner Store
by DyAnne DiSalvo-Ryan

 GO ONLINE For more resources, go to www.harcourtschool.com/ss1

304

For Your Reference

Atlas

R2 World Continents

R4 World Land and Water

R6 United States States and Capitals

R8 United States Land and Water

Research Handbook

R10

Biographical Dictionary

R18

Picture Glossary

R20

Index

R37

ATLAS

RESEARCH HANDBOOK

BIOGRAPHICAL DICTIONARY

PICTURE GLOSSARY

INDEX

World

Continents

ARCTIC OCEAN

NORTH AMERICA

PACIFIC OCEAN

ATLANTIC OCEAN

Equator

SOUTH AMERICA

PACIFIC OCEAN

SOUTHERN OCEAN

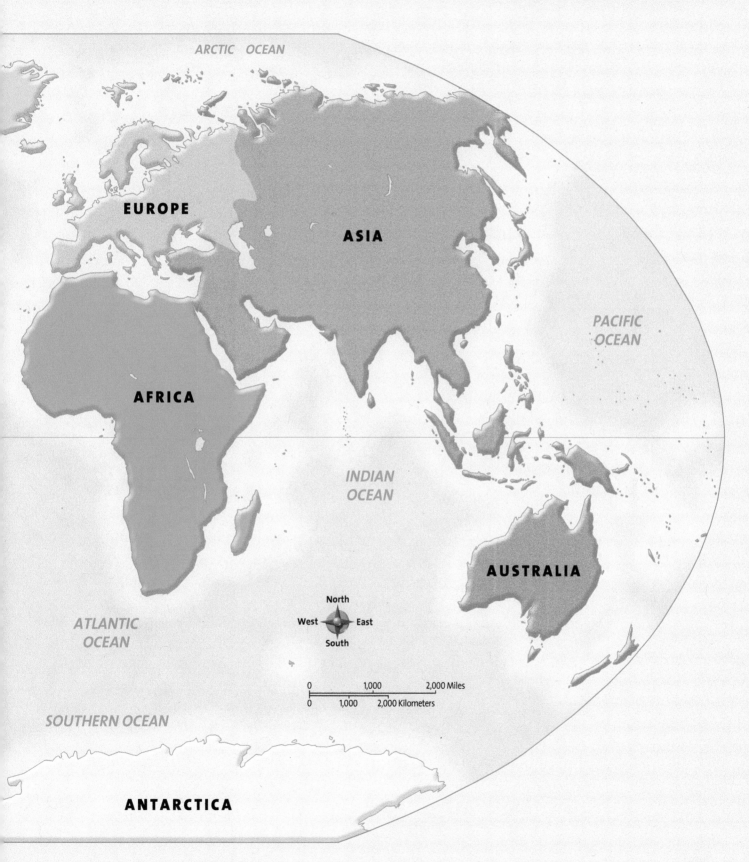

ARCTIC OCEAN

EUROPE

ASIA

AFRICA

PACIFIC
OCEAN

INDIAN
OCEAN

AUSTRALIA

ATLANTIC
OCEAN

North

West ─ East

South

0   1,000   2,000 Miles

0   1,000   2,000 Kilometers

SOUTHERN OCEAN

ANTARCTICA

R3

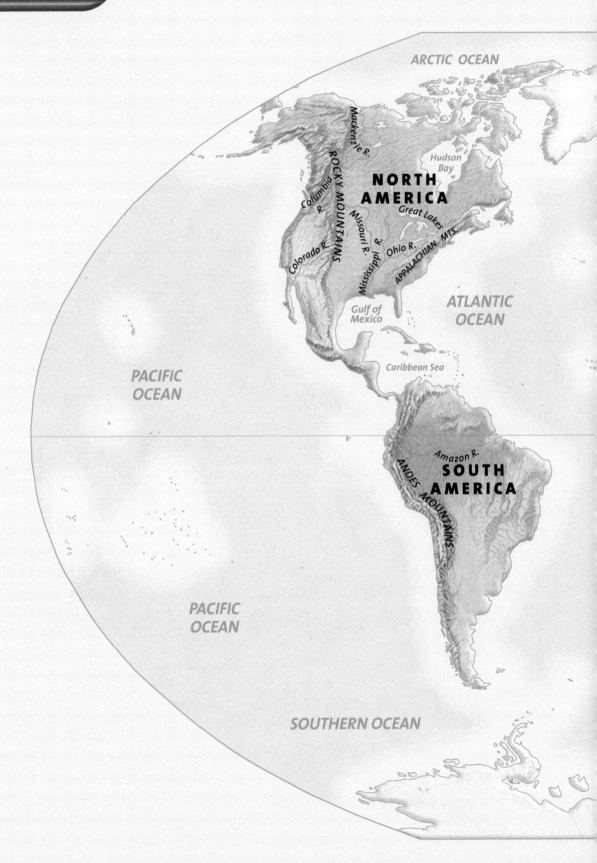

ARCTIC OCEAN

Mackenzie R.

Hudson
Bay

ROCKY MOUNTAINS

Columbia
R.

**NORTH
AMERICA**

Great Lakes

Missouri R.

Mississippi R.

Ohio R.

APPALACHIAN MTS.

Colorado R.

ATLANTIC
OCEAN

Gulf of
Mexico

PACIFIC
OCEAN

Caribbean Sea

Amazon R.

ANDES MOUNTAINS

**SOUTH
AMERICA**

PACIFIC
OCEAN

SOUTHERN OCEAN

Greenland

ARCTIC OCEAN

URAL MTS.

Volga R.

EUROPE

ASIA

Black Sea

Caspian Sea

Mediterranean Sea

Atlas Mts.

Sea of Okhotsk

GOBI (DESERT)

Huang He

HIMALAYAS

Chang Jiang

Nile R.

SAHARA

PACIFIC
OCEAN

Ganges R.

AFRICA

Arabian
Sea

Bay of
Bengal

South
China
Sea

Congo River

Lake Victoria

Lake
Tanganyika

Sumatra

INDIAN
OCEAN

New
Guinea

Madagascar

Kalahari
Desert

AUSTRALIA

GREAT VICTORIA
DESERT

Darling R.

ATLANTIC
OCEAN

Murray R.

North

West   East

South

0   1,000   2,000 Miles

0   1,000   2,000 Kilometers

SOUTHERN OCEAN

ANTARCTICA

R5

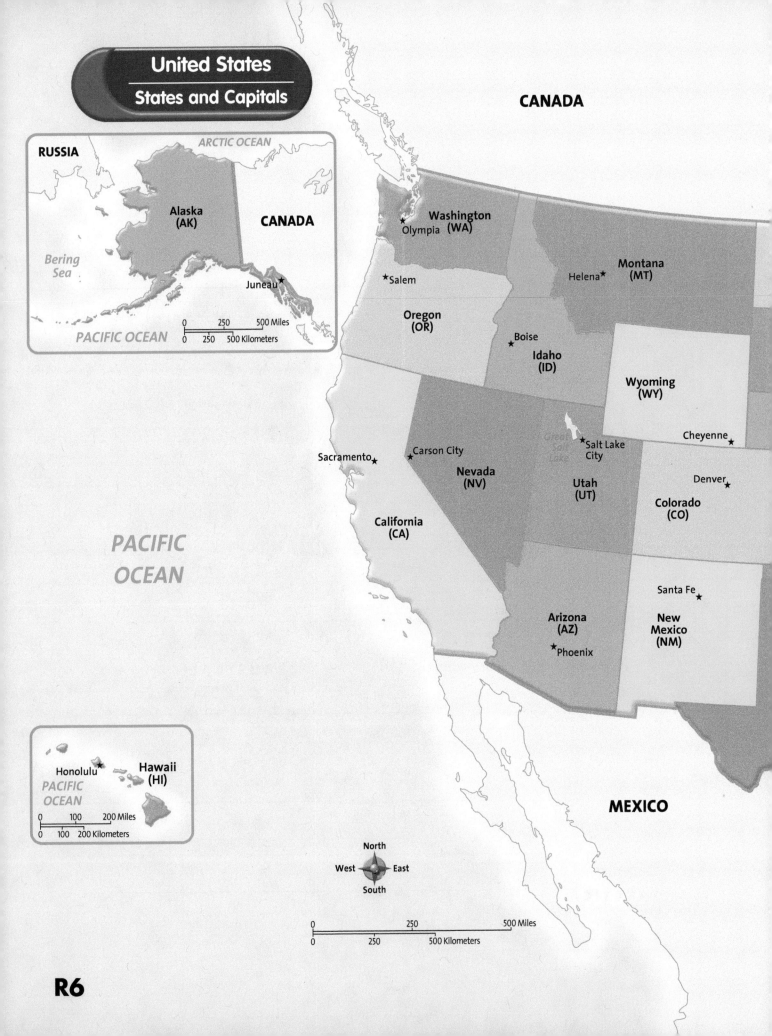

United States
States and Capitals

RUSSIA

ARCTIC OCEAN

Alaska
(AK)

CANADA

Bering
Sea

Juneau ★

PACIFIC OCEAN

0   250   500 Miles
0   250   500 Kilometers

CANADA

Washington
(WA)
Olympia ★

★ Salem

Oregon
(OR)

Helena ★

Montana
(MT)

Boise ★

Idaho
(ID)

Wyoming
(WY)

Cheyenne ★

PACIFIC
OCEAN

Sacramento ★

Carson City ★

Nevada
(NV)

California
(CA)

Great
Salt
Lake

★ Salt Lake
City

Utah
(UT)

Denver ★

Colorado
(CO)

Santa Fe ★

Arizona
(AZ)

★ Phoenix

New
Mexico
(NM)

Honolulu ★

Hawaii
(HI)

PACIFIC
OCEAN

0   100   200 Miles
0   100   200 Kilometers

North

West ◆ East

South

MEXICO

0   250   500 Miles
0   250   500 Kilometers

R6

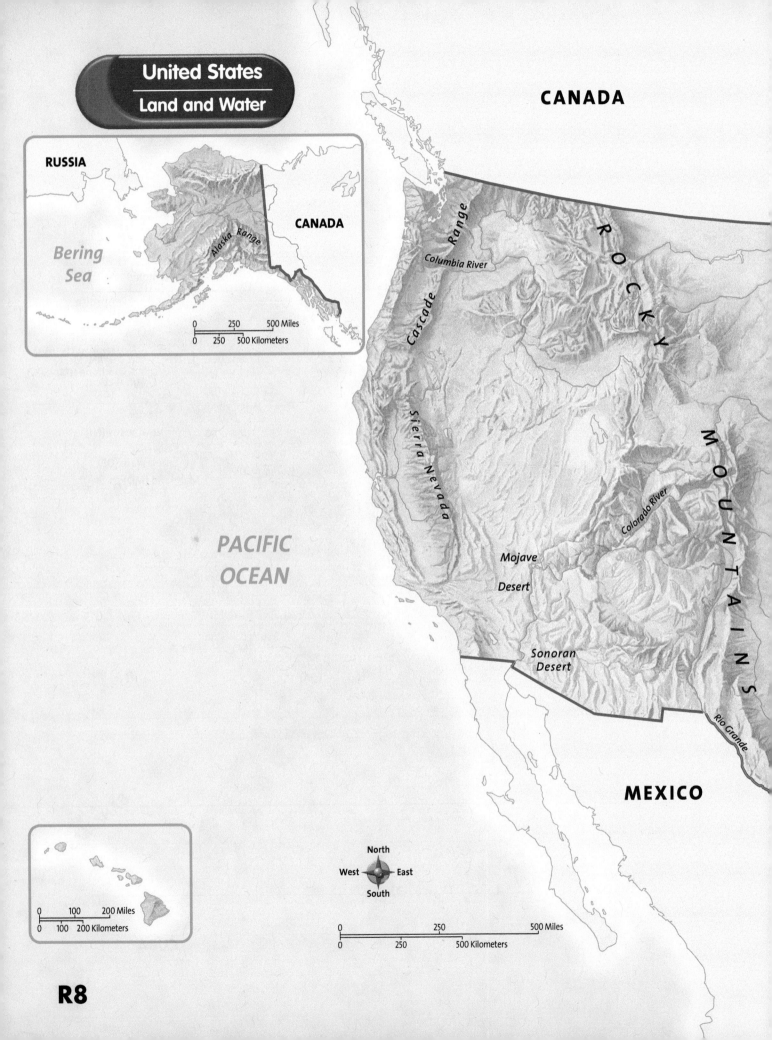

United States
Land and Water

RUSSIA

CANADA

Bering Sea

Alaska Range

0   250   500 Miles
0   250   500 Kilometers

CANADA

MEXICO

Columbia River

Cascade Range

R O C K Y

M O U N T A I N S

Sierra Nevada

Colorado River

Mojave Desert

Sonoran Desert

Rio Grande

PACIFIC OCEAN

0   100   200 Miles
0   100   200 Kilometers

North
West   East
South

0   250   500 Miles
0   250   500 Kilometers

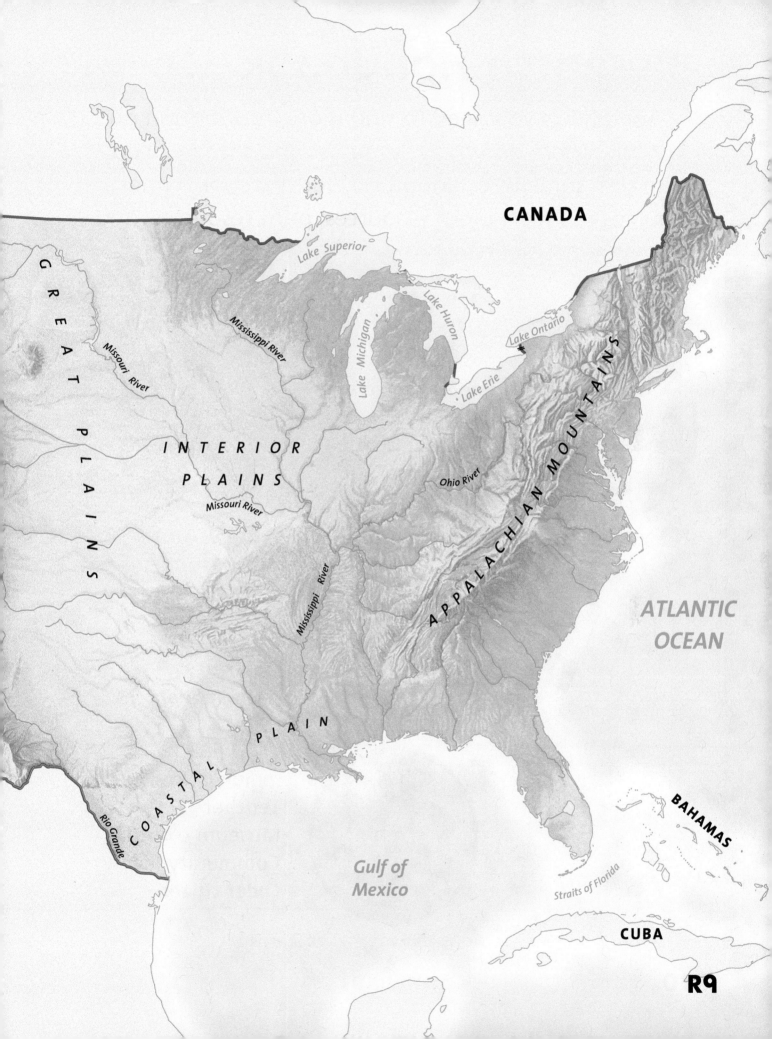

GREAT PLAINS

CANADA

Lake Superior

Lake Huron

Lake Michigan

Lake Ontario

Lake Erie

Missouri River

Mississippi River

INTERIOR
PLAINS

Missouri River

Ohio River

APPALACHIAN MOUNTAINS

Mississippi River

ATLANTIC
OCEAN

COASTAL PLAIN

Rio Grande

BAHAMAS

Gulf of
Mexico

Straits of Florida

CUBA

Research Handbook

Sometimes you need to find more information on a topic. There are many resources you can use. You can find some information in your textbook. Other sources are technology resources, print resources, and community resources.

Technology Resources
- Internet
- Computer disk
- Television or radio

Print Resources
- Atlas
- Dictionary
- Encyclopedia
- Nonfiction book
- Magazine or newspaper

Community Resources
- Teacher
- Museum curator
- Community leader
- Older citizen

Technology Resources

The main technology resources you can use are the Internet and computer disks. Television and radio can also be good sources of information.

Using the Internet

Information on the Internet is always changing. Be sure to use a site you can trust.

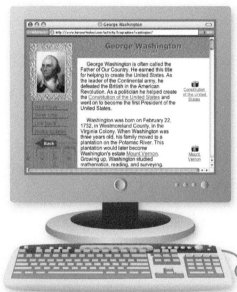

Finding Information

- Use a mouse and a keyboard to search for information.
- With help from a teacher, parent, or older child, find the source you want to search.
- Type in key words.
- Read carefully and take notes.
- If your computer is connected to a printer, you can print out a paper copy.

Print Resources

Books in libraries are placed in a special order. Each book has a call number. The call number tells you where to look for the book.

Some print resources, such as encyclopedias, magazines, and newspapers are kept together in a separate place. Librarians can help you find what you need.

Atlas

An atlas is a book of maps. Some atlases show the same place at different times.

Dictionary

A dictionary gives the correct spelling of words. It also tells you their definitions, or what they mean. Words in a dictionary are listed in alphabetical order. Guide words at the tops of the pages help you find the word you are looking for.

Guide Words

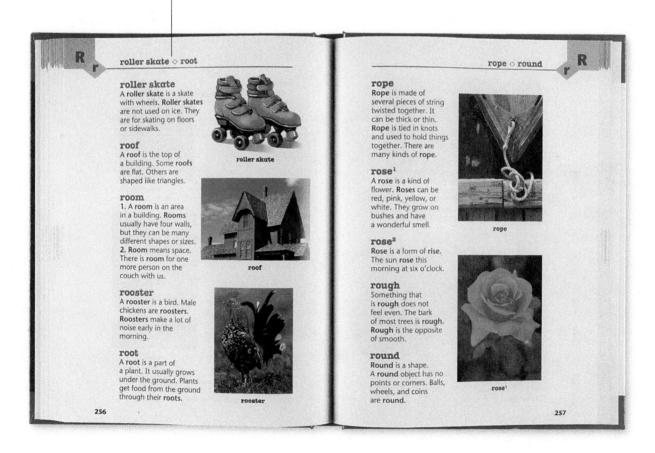

R r roller skate ◇ root

roller skate
A **roller skate** is a skate with wheels. **Roller skates** are not used on ice. They are for skating on floors or sidewalks.

roller skate

roof
A **roof** is the top of a building. Some **roofs** are flat. Others are shaped like triangles.

room
1. A **room** is an area in a building. **Rooms** usually have four walls, but they can be many different shapes or sizes.
2. **Room** means space. There is **room** for one more person on the couch with us.

roof

rooster
A **rooster** is a bird. Male chickens are **roosters**. **Roosters** make a lot of noise early in the morning.

root
A **root** is a part of a plant. It usually grows under the ground. Plants get food from the ground through their **roots**.

rooster

256

rope ◇ round **R** r

rope
Rope is made of several pieces of string twisted together. It can be thick or thin. **Rope** is tied in knots and used to hold things together. There are many kinds of **rope**.

rose¹
A **rose** is a kind of flower. **Roses** can be red, pink, yellow, or white. They grow on bushes and have a wonderful smell.

rope

rose²
Rose is a form of **rise**. The sun **rose** this morning at six o'clock.

rough
Something that is **rough** does not feel even. The bark of most trees is **rough**. **Rough** is the opposite of smooth.

round
Round is a shape. A **round** object has no points or corners. Balls, wheels, and coins are **round**.

rose¹

257

R13

Encyclopedia

An encyclopedia is a book or set of books that gives information about many different topics. The topics are listed in alphabetical order. An encyclopedia is a good source to use when beginning your research.

You can also find encyclopedias on the Internet. These encyclopedias might have sound and video clips.

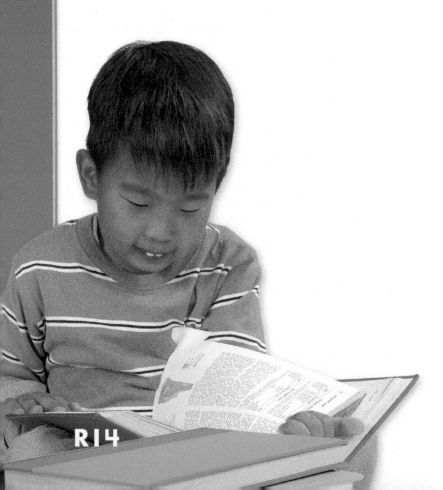

Nonfiction Books

A nonfiction book gives facts about real people, places, and things. Nonfiction books in the library are grouped by subject. Each subject has a different call number. Look in a card file or computer catalog to find a call number. You can look for titles, authors, or subjects.

HOME	SAVE RECORD	RETURN TO BROWSE	CHANGE SEARCH

TITLE | a | Kids Online | Search

Author	Florian, Douglas
Title	**A beach day / by Douglas Florian**
Edition	1st ed.
Publication info.	New York: Greenwillow Books, c1990
Description	32p.: col. ill.; 26 cm.
Summary	Describes simply how one family enjoys a day at the beach
Call number	E FLO

Magazines and Newspapers

Magazines and newspapers are printed by the day, week, or month. They are good sources of the latest information. Many libraries have a guide that lists articles by subject. Two guides are the <u>Children's Magazine Guide</u> and the <u>Readers' Guide to Periodical Literature</u>.

Community Resources

Often, people in your community can give you information you need. Before you talk to anyone, always ask a teacher or a parent for permission.

Listening to Find Information

Before

- Decide who to talk to.
- Make a list of useful questions.

During

- Be polite.
- Speak clearly and loudly.
- Listen carefully. You may think of other questions you want to ask.

- Take notes to help you remember ideas.
- Write down or tape record the person's exact words for quotes. Get permission to use the quotes.
- Later, write a thank-you letter.

Writing to Get Information

You can also write to people in your community to gather information. Keep these ideas in mind as you write:

- Write neatly or use a computer.
- Say who you are and why you are writing.
- Carefully check your spelling and punctuation.
- If you are mailing the letter, put in an addressed, stamped envelope for the person to send you an answer.
- Thank the person.

Biographical Dictionary

The Biographical Dictionary lists many of the important people introduced in this book. Names are listed in alphabetical (ABC) order by last name. After each name are the birth and death dates. If the person is still alive, only the birth year is given. The page number tells where the main discussion of each person starts.

Adams, **John** (1735–1826) Second President of the United States. He also served two terms as America's first Vice President. p. 112

Armstrong, **Neil** (1930–) First person to walk on the surface of the moon. p. 192

Boone, **Daniel** (1734–1820) American pathfinder who helped settle Kentucky. p. 88

Carver, **George Washington** (1864–1943) African American scientist and inventor. p. 82

Chavez, **Cesar** (1927–1993) Labor leader. He united many farmworkers to demand better treatment. p. 276

Cigrand, **Bernard** (1866–1932) Teacher and dentist. He is known as the founder of Flag Day. p. 136

Confucius (551 B.C.–479 B.C.) China's most famous teacher and philosopher. His personal goal was to encourage peace. p. 35

Franklin, **Benjamin** (1706–1790) American leader, writer, and inventor. He helped write the Declaration of Independence. p. 127

Key, **Francis Scott** (1779–1843) Lawyer and poet who wrote the words of "The Star-Spangled Banner." p. 119

King, **Martin Luther**, **Jr.** (1929–1968) African American minister and leader. He worked to win civil rights for all Americans. p. 130

Laird, **Addie** Child laborer. p. 271

Lincoln, **Abraham** (1809–1865) The 16th President of the United States. He was President during the Civil War. p. 130

Parker, **George S.** (1867–1953) One of the founders of a company that still makes popular games today. p. 174

Parks, **Rosa** (1913–2005) An African American civil rights leader. She refused to give up her seat on a bus to a white man. p. 40

Sacagawea (c. 1790–1812) Native American woman who helped Lewis and Clark explore parts of the United States. p. 218

Washington, **George** (1732–1799) First President of the United States. He is known as "The Father of Our Country." p. 110

Weaver, **Robert C.** (1907–1997) First African American to serve in the United States Cabinet. p. 226

Wilder, **Laura Ingalls** (1867–1957) Author. She wrote a series of books about her pioneer childhood. p. 70

Picture Glossary

The Picture Glossary has important words and their definitions. They are listed in alphabetical (ABC) order. The pictures help you understand the meanings of the words. The page number at the end tells where the word is first used.

B

ballot
A paper that shows all the choices in a vote. (page 26)

border
The place where a state or country ends. (page 58)

bar graph
A graph that uses bars to show how many or how much. (page 296)

business
The selling of goods or services. (page 269)

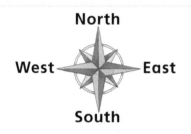

calendar

A chart that shows time. (page 134)

change

To become different. (page 170)

North

West — East

South

cardinal directions

The four main directions. (page 72)

citizen

A person who lives in and belongs to a community. (page 16)

celebration

A time to be happy about something special. (page 232)

city

A large community. (page 23)

colony

A land ruled by another country. (page 106)

continent

A large area of land. (page 60)

communication

The sharing of ideas and feelings. (page 162)

country

An area of land with its own people and laws. (page 58)

community

A group of people who live and work together. It is also the place where they live. (page 16)

culture

A group's way of life. (page 210)

custom
A group's way of doing something. (page 233)

Earth
Our planet. (page 60)

D

diagram
A picture that shows the parts of something. (page 124)

F

Fact The Liberty Bell was made in 1752.

fact
Something that is true and not made up. (page 190)

directions
The ways to places. (page 72)

factory
A building in which people use machines to make goods. (page 290)

fair
Acting in a way that is right and honest. (page 13)

flag
A piece of cloth with colors and shapes that stand for things. (page 116)

farm
A place for growing plants and raising animals. (page 69)

flowchart
A chart showing steps needed to make or do something. (page 216)

fiction
Stories that are made up. (page 190)

folktale
A story passed from person to person. (page 228)

freedom
The right people have to make their own choices. (page 108)

goods
Things that people make or grow to sell. (page 260)

future
The time that is to come. (page 181)

government
A group of people who lead a community. (page 24)

 G

globe
A model of Earth. (page 60)

government service
Services the government does for the community. (page 28)

governor

The leader of a state government. (page 24)

H

hero

A person who does something brave or important to help others. (page 129)

history

The story of what happened in the past. (page 212)

I

immigrant

A person from another part of the world who has come to live in this country. (page 220)

J

job

Work that a person does to earn money. (page 268)

L

landmark

A symbol that is a place people can visit. (page 122)

language

A group's way of speaking. (page 213)

location

The place where something is. (page 56)

law

A rule that people in a community must follow. (page 17)

M

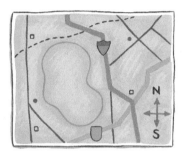

map

A picture that shows where places are. (page 20)

leader

A person who is in charge of a group. (page 22)

map key

Shows what each symbol on a map stands for. (page 20)

market

A place where people buy and sell goods. (page 280)

national holiday

A day to honor a person or an event that is important to our country. (page 128)

mayor

The leader of a city. (page 23)

neighborhood

A part of a town or city. (page 68)

money

What people use to pay for goods and services. (page 262)

nonfiction

Stories about real things. (page 190)

PICTURE GLOSSARY

R28

O

ocean

A large body of water. (page 60)

plain

Land that is mostly flat. (page 63)

 P

past

The time before now. (page 178)

pledge

A kind of promise. (page 118)

picture graph

A graph that uses pictures to show how many there are of something. (page 264)

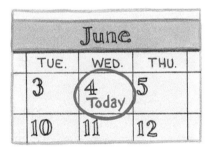

present

The time now. (page 179)

R

President

The leader of the
United States.
(page 26)

recreation
What people do for
fun. (page 87)

principal

The leader of a
school. (page 12)

recycle

To make something
old into something
new. (page 79)

problem

Something that is
hard to solve, or fix.
(page 14)

religion

A belief in a god or
gods. (page 229)

PICTURE GLOSSARY

resource

Anything that people can use. (page 74)

right

Something people are free to do. (page 36)

respect

To treat someone or something well. (page 34)

role

The part a person plays in a group or community. (page 239)

responsibility

Something that people should do. (page 11)

route

A way to go from one place to another. (page 236)

rule

An instruction that tells people how to act. (page 10)

season

A time of year. (page 85)

save

To keep something, such as money, to use later. (page 284)

services

Kinds of work people do for others for money. (page 262)

scarce

Not enough of something. (page 286)

settler

A person who makes a home in a new place. (page 104)

share
To use something with others. (page 38)

sportsmanship
Playing fairly. (page 38)

shelter
A home. (page 70)

state
A part of a country. (page 57)

solution
An answer to a problem. (page 14)

symbol
A picture or object that stands for something. (page 20)

T

table

A chart that shows things in groups. (page 176)

time line

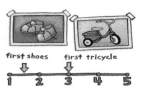

first shoes   first tricycle

1   2   3   4   5

A line that shows the order in which things have happened. (page 182)

teacher

A person who leads the class. (page 10)

today

This day. (page 134)

technology

All of the tools we use to make our lives easier. (page 186)

tomorrow

The day after today. (page 134)

tool
Something a person uses to do work. (page 166)

valley
Low land between mountains. (page 63)

trade
To give one thing to get another. (page 282)

volunteer
A person who works without pay to help people. (page 273)

transportation
Any way of moving people and things. (page 71)

vote
A choice that gets counted. (page 26)

wants

Things people would like to have. (page 286)

world

All the people and places on Earth. (page 220)

weather

The way the air feels outside. (page 84)

yesterday

The day before today. (page 134)

Index

The index tells where information about people, places, and events in this book can be found. The entries are listed in alphabetical order. Each entry tells the page or pages where you can find the topic.

Adams, John, 112, R18
Address, 110
Africa, 61
African Americans, 40–41, 130, 226
Alabama, 40–41
Algeria, 240
America, first people in, 210–215
"America" (Smith), 102–103
American heroes, 128–133
American Indians. See Native Americans
American Revolution, 108–109
American symbols, 97, 100–101, 102–103, 116–119, 120–125, 138–139
Antarctica, 61
Appalachian Mountains, 66
Arctic Ocean, 61
Armstrong, Neil, 192–193, R18
Art, 227
Artifacts, 214, 224
Asia, 61
Astronaut, 192–193
Atlantic Ocean, 61, 65, 104
Atlas, R2–R9, R12

Aunt Flossie's Hats (Howard), 150–157
Australia, 61
Azalea Festival, 161

B

Bald eagle, 100–101, 121, 139, 141
Ballot, 26–27
Bank, 284
Bar graph, 296–297, 303
Beach, 45, 88
Beliefs, 228–229, 231, 244
Biography
  Armstrong, Neil, 192–193
  Carver, George Washington, 82–83
  Chavez, Cesar, 276–277
  Parks, Rosa, 40–41
  Sacagawea, 218–219
  Washington, George, 110–111
Boone, Daniel, 88, R18
Border, 58–59, 61, 66, 93
Boston Light, 52
Brazil, 206–209
Business, 269, 273, 284, 298–299
Butterflies, 88
Buyers, 261, 280–285, 288–289

Calendar, 134–135
California, 185
  Death Valley, 86
Camera, 169
Canada, 224
Capital, R6–R7
Capitol, 24, 122, 138–139, 143
Cardinal directions, 72, 95
Caring, 82–83
Carver, George Washington, 82–83, R18
Categorize, 52–53, 92
Cause, 4–5, 44
Celebrations, 128–133, 232–235
Change, 147, 170, 194–195
  jobs and, 180–181
  technology and, 184–189
  time and, 178–179, 182–183
Character
  caring, 82–83
  fairness, 276–277
  patriotism, 192–193
  respect, 40–41
  responsibility, 218–219
  trustworthiness, 110–111

Chart and Graph Skills
  bar graph, 296
  calendar, 134
  diagram, 124
  flowchart, 216
  picture graph, 264
  put things in groups, 176
  time line, 182
Chavez, Cesar, 276–277, R18
Cherokee Indians, 211, 212–213
Cherry Hill, New Jersey, 110
Children, 278–279
Children in History
  Laird, Addie, 271, R19
  Parker, George S., 174, R19
  Wilder, Laura Ingalls, 70, R19
China, 35, 224
Chinese Lantern, How to Make a, 246
Chinese New Year, 232–233
Chlodnik, 204
Choices, 108, 281, 286
  buying, 286–287
  recreation, 87
  voting, 3, 26–27
Chumash Indians, 216–217
Cigrand, Bernard, 136, R18
Cinco de Mayo, 234
Citizens, 16, 19, 45, 140
  character traits of, 40–41, 82–83, 110–111, 192–193, 218–219, 276–277
  honoring, 128–130
  responsibilities of, 37
  rights of, 36–37

Citizenship
  Flag Day, 136–137
  Helping Others, 278–279
  Police Officers and You, 32–33
Citizenship Skills
  voting, 26–27
  working together, 38–39
City, 23, 57, 68–69, 113
City Hall, 42–43
Clark, Captain William, 218–219
Classify, 52–53, 92
Cleveland, Ohio, 68
Clinton, William J., 41
Clothespins, 167
Clothing, 86, 92, 159, 222, 240
  long ago, 146, 159, 164, 194
  today, 146, 195
Colony, 106–107, 113
Communication, 162–163
Communities, 2, 16, 19, 42–43, 45, 68–69, 89, 96
  changes in, 178–181
  different cultures in, 220–223, 226–227
  history of, 178–181
  honoring their citizens, 128–131
  laws of, 3, 16–19, 32–33
  leaders in, 22–25
  long ago, 178–181
  responsibilities of citizens in, 37
Compare, 204–205, 244
Confucius, 35, R18
Congressional Gold Medal, 41
Conservation, 80–81

Constitution Day, 132
Constitution, United States, 100, 109, 115, 127, 142
Continent, 51, 60–61, 94, R2–R5
Contrast, 204–205, 244
Country, 50, 58–59, 220–225
  leader of, 26–27
  map of, 58
Crayon factory, 290–295
Crayons, 290–295
Critical Thinking Skills
  buying, 286–287
  solve a problem, 14–15
  tell fact from fiction, 190–191
Culture, 202, 220–223, 245
  celebrations and, 226, 232–235
  defined, 202, 210
  expressing, 228–231
  festival of, 226
  learning about, 228–231
  of Native Americans, 210–215
  sharing, 215, 222, 225
Customs, 203, 233–235, 245

Dam, 77
Dance, 223, 230–231
Days, 134, 182
Death Valley, 86
Declaration of Independence, 100, 107, 109, 114, 127
Delaware Indians, 211
Deserts, 114, 62–63, 86

Detail, 100–101, 140
Detroit, Michigan, 269, 288
Diagram, 124–125, 143
Directions, 72
 cardinal, 72
 on maps, 72–73, 95
Diversity, 204–205, 220–225, 226–227, 232–235
Documents, 100, 107
 Constitution of the United States, 100, 109, 115, 127, 132, 142
 Declaration of Independence, 100, 107, 114, 127
 John Adams's journal, 112

E

Earlier generations, 158–163
 communication, 162–163
 dress, 159
 festivals, 161
 games, 174
 home tools, 166–169
 work, 160
Earth, I8–I10, 60, 74–75, 78–79, 188, 193, 220
East, 72, 95
Effect, 4–5, 44
Eggbeater, 166
El Salvador, 221, 223
Elkhart, Indiana, 178–181
Ellis Island, New York, 224
E-mail, 163

Emans, Elaine V., 54–55
England, 104–109
Europe, 61, 104
Exchange, 282, 285
Exploration, 218–219
Explorers, 218–219

F

Fact, 190–191
Factory, 251, 290–295, 301
Fair, 13, 106
Fair play, 38–39
Fairness, 276–277
Fall, 85
Families
 around the world, 238–241
 interviewing members of, 163
 long ago, 158–163, 164–165
Farm, 69, 90–91, 94
Farmers, 82–83, 288–289
Farmworkers, 276–277
Fayetteville, Tennesee, 69
Festivals, 161, 226, 232–233
Fiction, 190–191
Field Trip
 Great Smoky Mountains National Park, 66–67
 Liberty Bell, 126–127
 Royal Oak Farmers Market, 288–289
Fire station, 42–43
Firefighters, 29, 42–43
Flag, 98, 116–119, 136–137, 141, 193
Flag Day, 136–137

Flowchart, 216–217, 246, 283
Folktale, 206–209, 228–231, 242–243
Folktales
 "How Beetles Became Beautiful" (a folktale from Brazil), 206–209
Food, 75–77, 89, 204, 210–211, 217, 220, 222, 226–227, 240–241
Ford, M. Lucille, 6–9
Forest, I14, 66
Fort McHenry, 52
Fourth of July (Independence Day), 107, 132, 141
Franklin, Benjamin, 107, 127, 285, R19
Franklin Court, 127
Freedom, 98, 100, 108, 111, 112–115, 126
 of religion, 36
 of speech, 36
Free-market economy, 260–265
Friendship, 6–9
"Friendship's Rule" (Ford), 6–9
Fruit, 76, 288–289
Fun with Social Studies, 42–43, 90–91, 138–139, 194–195, 242–243, 298–299
Future, 181

G

Games, 161, 174
Gateway Arch, 123
Geography, I8–I14, R12
 five themes of, I8–I9
 review, I10–I13
 terms, I14

Globe, 51, 60–61, 93
  drawing of, 61
Golden Rule, 35, 39
Goods, 250, 260–263, 266–267, 280, 301
  trading, 282, 300
Government, 24, 41, 45
  choosing leaders of, 24, 26–27
  services, 28–31
  workers, 28–31
Governor, 24
Grand Canyon National Park, 52
Graphs
  bar, 296–297, 303
  picture, 264–265, 302
Great Smoky Mountains National Park, 66–67
  Cades Cove, 67
Groups, 15, 22, 36, 238–239, 276–277, 278–279
  putting things in, 176–177
  working together in, 38–39
Gulf, 114

Hackensack, New Jersey, 213
Heo, Yumi, 254–259
Hermann, Missouri, 69
Heroes, 99, 129–130, 141
Highway, 30
Hill, 114, 62
Historic places, 52–53
  Boston Light, 52
  Fort McHenry, 52
  Independence National Historical Park, 126

History, 104–109, 110–111, 112–115, 166–169, 170–175, 184–189, 202, 210–215, 218–219
  learning about, 158–163, 212–213
Holidays, 128–133, 136–137
Home tools, 166–169, 194–195
Homes, 70, 165
Hot Springs National Park, 52
Houses, 70
"How Beetles Became Beautiful" (a folktale from Brazil), 206–209
Howard, Elizabeth Fitzgerald, 150–157
Hupa Indians, 215

Icons
  Rosie the Riveter, 266
  Sacagawea, 218–219
Immigrants, 203, 220–225
Independence Day (Fourth of July), 132, 141
Independence Hall, 106–107, 127
Independence National Historical Park, 126–127
India, 220
Indian Ocean, 61
Indiana, 57
Indians, American. See Native Americans
Interview, 163, R16
Internet, R11

Ireland, 224
Iron, 167
Island, 114, 124–125
Italy, 224

Japan, 239
Jobs, 268–273, 274–275, 291, 295
Jonesborough, Tenessee, 16–17

Kentucky, 24, 88
Kenya, 221
Key, Francis Scott, 119, R19
King, Martin Luther, Jr., 130, 141–142, R19
K-W-L chart, 274–275

Labor Day, 133
Laird, Addie, 271, R19
Lake, 114, 64, 89
Land, 62–63
  on maps, 56–59, 60–61, R4–R5, R8–R9
  as a resource, 74–76
  symbols for, 59
  types of, 62–63
Landmarks, 99, 122–123, 124–125, 141
Language, 204–205, 213
Lantern Festival, 233

Laws, 3, 17–19, 41
  breaking, 19
  of communities, 16–19
  and respect, 37
Leaders, 22–25
  of cities, 23
  of communities, 22–25
  of countries, 26, 110–111
  of schools, 10, 12
  of states, 24
  of the United States, 26, 111
Learning, 170–175
Lemonade, 298–299
Lemons, 298–299
Lewis, Captain Meriwether, 218–219
Lewis and Clark, 218–219
Liberty Bell, 120, 126, 138–139
Liberty Island, 124–125
Librarians, 31, 42–43
Library, 31, 42–43, R12–R15
Lincoln, Abraham, 130, R19
Lincoln Monument 130
Literature
  "America" (Smith), 102–103
  Aunt Flossie's Hats (Howard), 150–157
  "Friendship's Rule" (Ford), 6–9
  "How Beetles Became Beautiful" (a folktale from Brazil), 206–209
  "Making Maps" (Emans), 54–55
  One Afternoon (Heo), 254–259
Location, 56–59

M

Main Idea, 100–101, 140
"Making Maps" (Emans), 54–55
Map and Globe Skills,
  directions, 72
  follow a route, 236
  globe, 60
  read a map, 20
Map key, 20–21
Map symbols, 20–21
Maps, 111, 112–113, 20–21, 54–55, 56–59, 95
  find capitals, cities, and states on, 57, 58, R6–R7
  locate the seven continents on, 61, R2–R3
  of countries, 58, 220–221
  find directions on, 72–73, 95
  Indiana, 57
  Kentucky, 24
  showing land and water on, 59, 61, R4–R5, R8–R9
  route of Mayflower, 104
  of Native American territories, 214
  of a neighborhood, 111, 20–21, 46, 56
  locate the four oceans on, 61, R2–R3
  Oklahoma, 59
  follow routes on, 236–237, 247
  of a school, 113
  symbols on, 20–21
  the 13 colonies, 106, 113
  of the United States, 58, R2–R3, R6–R9
  of the world, 61, 94, R2–R5
  of a zoo, 95
Market, 251, 280–281, 285, 288–289, 298–299, 301
Martin Luther King, Jr., Day, 130, 142
Mayflower (ship), 104–105
Mayor, 23, 25
Medicine, 180
Memorial Day, 128
Mexico, 204–205, 224, 234
  tortillas, 204
Milkman, 166
Missouri, 69, 185
Model, 60
Money, 121, 138–139, 262–263, 283–285, 298–299
  earning, 268, 273
  How Money Moves (chart), 283
  saving, 284–285
  spending, 262, 281–282, 283–285, 286, 300
  symbol of United States, 121
  trading, 282, 285, 298–299, 300
Mongolia, 240
Montgomery, Alabama, 41
Months, 134, 182
Monuments, 99, 120, 122, 130, 138–139
Moon, 189, 193
Mount Rushmore, 99, 122

Mountain, 114, 62, 66, 88
Murals, 227
Music, 227
Musical instruments, 181

NASA, 192–193
Nashville, Tennessee, 52
National holidays, 99, 128–133, 136–137, 141
National parks, 52–53
  Grand Canyon National Park, 52
  Great Smoky Mountains National Park, 66–67
  Hot Springs National Park, 52
  Independence National Historical Park, 126–127
Native Americans, 210–215
  artifacts of, 214
  culture of, 210, 213, 215
  and early explorers, 218–219
  and early settlers, 214–215
  language of, 213
  as storytellers, 212
  territory of, 214
  tribes of, 210–211, 216–217, 218
Nature, caring for, 78–79, 82–83
Navajo Indians, 211
Navy, United States, 129, 192
Needs, 240–241
Neighborhood, 68
  map of, 111, 20–21, 46

New Year's celebration, 232–233
New Year's Day, 142
New York City, 52–53, 278–279
Nez Perce Indians, 210
Nonfiction, 190–191
North, 72, 95
North America, 61, 104–106, 210
  exploration of, 104–106, 218–219
  map of, R2–R5
North Carolina, 66, 161

Ocean, 114, 60–61, 64–65, 104, 224
  Atlantic, 61, 65, 104
  Pacific, 61, 65
Oklahoma, 59
One Afternoon (Heo), 254–259

Pacific Ocean, 61, 65
Park rangers, 30, 42–43
Parker, George S., 174, R19
Parks, Rosa, 40–41, R19
Past, 146, 178, 181, 197–198
Patriotic symbols, 100–101, 120–123
Patriotism, 116–119, 128–133, 192–193
Peanuts, 83
Peninsula, 114
Philadelphia, Pennsylvania, 106, 113, 126–127

Phonograph, 169
Physical environment, 52, 62–71, 74–81, 88–89
Picture graph, 264–265, 302
Pilgrims, 105, 131, 141
Pioneer, 70
Plain, 114, 63
Plants, 67, 82–83
  "the plant doctor," 82
Pledge, 116–119, 140
Pledge of Allegiance, 116–119, 140
Poetry
  "Friendship's Rule" (Ford), 6–9
  "Making Maps" (Emans), 54–55
Points of View, 88–89, 226–227, 266–267
Poland, 204–205
  Chlodnik, 204
Police Activities League (PAL), 33
Police officers, 29, 32–33, 42–43
Police station, 42–43
Pony Express, 185
Potato masher, 166
Present, 146, 179, 197–198
President, 26, 109, 110–111, 112, 130
  the first, of United States, 109, 110–111, 130
Presidents' Day, 130
Primary Sources
  Home Tools, 166–169
  Learning About Freedom, 112–115
Principal, 12–13, 42–43
Problem, 14
Problem solving, 14–15

Radio, 168
Reading Social Studies Skills
  Categorize and Classify, 52–53
  Cause and Effect, 4–5
  Compare and Contrast, 204–205
  Main Idea and Details, 100–101
  Recall and Retell, 252–253
  Sequence, 148–149
Recall, 252–253, 300
Recreation, 87, 93, 222
Recycle, 79, 81
Refrigerator, 166
Religion, 229, 231
  freedom of, 36, 45
Resources, 51, 74, 79, 90–91, 93
  saving, 78–79
  types of, 74, 79, 93
  uses of, 74–77, 79
Respect, 34–37, 38, 40–41
Responsibility, 11, 13, 37, 45, 78, 218–219
Retell, 252–253, 300
Rights, 36–37
Rivers, 114, 64, 89
  "mouth of a river," 213
Role, 203, 239, 245
Rose, 121
Rosie the Riveter, 266
Route, 236–237, 247
Royal Oak Farmers Market, 288–289
Rules, 3, 10, 32–33
  in a community, 16–19
  at school, 10–13
  of the United States, 109
Russia, 221, 223–224

Sacagawea, 218–219, R19
Save, 284
Saving money, 284–285
Scarce, 286
School resource officer, 32
Schools
  alike and different, 170–175
  going to, 175
  leaders of, 10, 12
  long ago, 148–149, 170–175
  map of, 112–113
  rules at, 10–13, 44
  today, 171, 175
  tools used in, 172–173, 177
  workers at, 10, 12, 31, 32, 42–43
Seasons, 85, 87
Sellers, 261, 262, 280, 282, 285, 288–289
Sequence, 148–149, 196
Services, 250, 262, 266–267, 301
  government, 28–31
  trading, 282, 283, 300
  types of, 262–263
Settlers, 88, 104–105, 214–215
Sewing machine, 167
Share, 38, 223
Shelter, 70–71, 240

Shoshone Indians, 218
Smith, Samuel F., 102–103
Social practices, 210–215, 222–223, 225, 226–227, 232–235
Soil, 74–75, 83, 93
Solution, 14
Solving problems, 14–15
Songs
  "America" (Smith), 102–103
  "Star-Spangled Banner, The" (Key), 119
South, 72, 95
South Africa, 239
South America, 61
Southern Ocean, 61, 94
Space, 188, 192–193
Space shuttle, 188–189
Special times, 232–235
Speech, freedom of, 36, 45
Sportsmanship, 38
Spring, 85
"Star-Spangled Banner, The" (Key), 119
State, 50, 57–59
  first in United States, 106
  flag of, 116
  leader of, 24
  on maps, 58, R6–R7
  parks, 52
Statue of Liberty, 124–125, 138–139
  diagram of, 125
Stories
  Aunt Flossie's Hats (Howard), 150–157
  One Afternoon (Heo), 254–259
Storytelling, 212–213, 228

Study Skills
  Build Vocabulary,
    80–81
  Preview and Question,
    274–275
  Use Visuals, 164–165
Summer, 85, 88
Symbols, 20, 100,
    120–123
  for land and water
    on maps, 59, R2–R9
  on maps, 20–21,
    R2–R9
  of the United States,
    98–99, 100, 116–119,
    120–123, 124–125,
    126–127

Table, 176–177
Teacher, 10, 31, 42–43,
    82–83
Technology, 145, 147,
    186–189, 197
  change and, 145,
    186–189
  for communication,
    162–163
  home tools, 166–169
  for transportation,
    145, 184–189
Telephone, 162, 168
Television, 169
Tennessee, 52, 66, 69
Terre Haute, Indiana,
    57
Thanksgiving Day, 131
Theme parks, 52–53
  Disneyland, 52
  SeaWorld, 52
  Six Flags, 52
Thirteen colonies, The,
    106, 109, 113

Time line, 41, 83, 111,
    147, 182–183, 193, 197,
    199, 219, 277
Today, 134
Tomorrow, 134
Tools, 166
  home, 166–169
  long ago, 166–169,
    172–173, 176–177
  today, 176–177
Tortillas, 204
Town, 69, 94
Trade, 251, 282, 285,
    298–299, 301
Transportation, 71,
    184–189
  books about, 190–191
  of goods, 71, 291
  long ago, 184–189,
    196, 198
  modes of, 71, 89,
    184–189, 198
  Pony Express, 185
  today, 188–189
Trustworthiness, 110–111
Typewriter, 168

Union, 276–277
**United Farm Workers of
America**, 276–277
**United States of
America, The**, 58
  exploration of, 218–
    219
  first President of, 109,
    110–111, 130
  first states of, 106
  flag of, 98, 116–119
  history of, 104–109,
    110–111, 112–115,
    126–127, 210–215,
    218–219, 224

  law in, 226
  leaders of, 24, 26–27,
    130
  maps of, 58, 113,
    R6–R9
  Pledge of Allegiance
    to, 116–119, 140
  songs about, 102–103,
    119
  symbols of, 98–99,
    100, 116–119, 120–
    123, 124–125, 126–127
**United States
Constitution**, 100, 109,
    115, 127, 132, 142

Valley, 114, 63, 65
Vegetables, 75, 288–289
Veterans Day, 128
Volunteer, 273, 278–279
Vote, 3, 26–27, 45, 47

W

Wampanoag Indians,
    105, 131
Wants, 286
War, 108–109, 141, 266
  marching drum, 108
Washer, 167
Washington, George,
    108–109, 110–111, 115,
    130, R19
Washington Monument,
    99, 122, 138–139, 141
Water
  on maps, R4–R5, R8–
    R9
  as a resource, 74, 77,
    81, 93

symbols for, 59, R4–R5, R8–R9

types of, 64–65

uses of, 77

Weather, 84–87, 92

Weaver, Robert C., 226, R19

Weeks, 134, 182

West, 72, 95

Wilder, Laura Ingalls, 70, R19

Wilderness Road, The, 88

Wildflowers, 67

Wilmington, North Carolina, 161

Winter, 85, 88

Work, 252, 260–263, 268, 272–275

inside and outside the home, 160

Workers

children, 271

factory, 271, 290–295

farm, 276–277

government, 28–31

inside and outside the home, 160

military, 129

Rosie the Riveter, 266

school, 10, 12, 31

strike, 277

union, 276–277

women, 160, 266

Working together, 14, 38–39

World, 220, 225

maps of, 61, 94, R2–R5

Years, 134, 182

Yesterday, 134

For permission to reprint copyrighted material, grateful acknowledgment is made to the following sources:

Belitha Press Limited: Cover illustration by Terry Hadler from *Traveling Through Time: Trains* by Neil Morris. Illustration copyright © 1997 by Belitha Press Limited.

Candlewick Press, Inc.: Cover illustration by Peter Joyce from *The Once Upon a Time Map Book* by B. G. Hennessy. Illustration copyright © 1999 by Peter Joyce.

Capstone Press: Cover illustration from *Flag Day* by Mari C. Schuh. Copyright © 2003 by Capstone Press.

The Child's World®, www.childsworld.com: Cover illustration by Mechelle Ann from *The Child's World of Responsibility* by N. Pemberton and J. Riehecky. Copyright © 1998 by The Child's World®, Inc.

Chronicle Books LLC, San Francisco, CA: From *Amazing Aircraft* by Seymour Simon. Text copyright © 2002 by Seymour Simon.

Clarion Books/Houghton Mifflin Company: From *Aunt Flossie's Hats (and Crab Cakes Later)* by Elizabeth Fitzgerald Howard, illustrated by James Ransome. Text copyright © 1991, 2001 by Elizabeth Fitzgerald Howard; illustrations copyright © 1991 by James Ransome.

Coward-McCann, A Division of Penguin Young Readers Group, A Member of Penguin Group (USA) Inc., 345 Hudson St., New York, NY 10014: Cover illustration by Paul Galdone from *George Washington's Breakfast* by Jean Fritz. Illustration copyright © 1969 by Paul Galdone.

Dial Books for Young Readers, A Division of Penguin Young Readers Group, A Member of Penguin Group (USA) Inc., 345 Hudson St., New York, NY 10014: Cover illustration by Jose Aruego & Ariane Dewey from *How Chipmunk Got His Stripes: A Tale of Bragging and Teasing* by Joseph Bruchac & James Bruchac. Illustration copyright © 2001 by Jose Aruego & Ariane Dewey.

Dorling Kindersley Limited, London: From *The Random House Children's Encyclopedia.* Text copyright © 1991 by Dorling Kindersley Ltd. Originally published under the title *The Dorling Kindersley Children's Illustrated Encyclopedia,* 1991.

Free Spirit Publishing Inc., Minneapolis, MN, 1-866-703-7322, www.freespirit.com: Cover illustration by Meredith Johnson from *Know and Follow Rules* by Cheri J. Meiners, M. Ed. Illustration copyright © 2005 by Free Spirit Publishing Inc.

Groundwood Books Ltd., Canada: Illustrations by Ian Wallace from *The Name of the Tree* by Celia Barker Lottridge. Illustrations copyright © 1989 by Ian Wallace.

Harcourt, Inc.: From *Sometimes* by Keith Baker. Copyright © 1999 by Harcourt, Inc.

HarperCollins Publishers: Cover and illustration by Kevin O'Malley from *Chanukah in Chelm* by David A. Adler. Illustrations copyright © 1997 by Kevin O'Malley. Cover illustration from *Grandpa's Corner Store* by DyAnne DiSalvo-Ryan. Copyright © 2000 by DyAnne DiSalvo-Ryan.

Herald Press: Cover illustration from *Henner's Lydia* by Marguerite de Angeli. Copyright © 1936, renewed 1964 by Marguerite de Angeli.

Ideals Publications, www.IdealsPublications.com: Cover illustration by Nancy Munger from *The Story of "The Star-Spangled Banner"* by Patricia A. Pingry. Illustration copyright © 2005 by Nancy Munger and Ideals Publications.

me + mi publishing, inc.: Cover illustration by Ann Iosa from *Jobs Around My Neighborhood/Oficios en mi vecindario* by Gladys Rosa-Mendoza. Copyright © 2002 by me + mi publishing, inc.

Scholastic Inc.: Cover and illustration from *One Grain of Rice: A Mathematical Folktale* by Demi. Copyright © 1997 by Demi. "Making Maps" by Elaine V. Emans and "Friendship's Rule" by M. Lucille Ford from *Poetry Place Anthology.* Text copyright © 1983 by Edgell Communications. *One Afternoon* by Yumi Heo. Copyright © 1994 by Yumi Heo. Published by Orchard Books/Scholastic Inc.

PHOTO CREDITS GRADE 1 SOCIAL STUDIES 2010 B PRINTING

PLACEMENT KEY: (t) top; (b) bottom; (l) left; (r) right; (c) center; (bg) background; (fg) foreground (i) inset

COVER: (bg) The Image Bank/Getty Images; (bl) Robert Dowling/Corbis; (cl) Rubberball/Getty Images

FRONTMATTER: [i] (bg) The Image Bank/Getty Images; [i] (c) Bob Rowan; Progressive Image/CORBIS; v (bg) Tony Freeman/PhotoEdit; vii (b) Dave Bartruff/Photolibrary; (cr) ThinkStock LLC/Getty Images; ix (b) PhotoLink/Photodisc/Getty Images; (tr) Leif Skoogfors/Corbis; x (r) Photolibrary; xi (cr) Museum of Flight/Corbis; (bl) Robert Maust/Photo Agora; xiii (b) Jonathan Nourok/PhotoEdit; I1 (tr) Jim Cummins/Getty Images; I2 (tl) Corbis; I3 (tl) Gary Conner/PhotoEdit; (br) Woodplay of Tampa; I8 (br) Getty Images; (cl) Photodisc/Getty Images; I9 (cr) Imagestate; (t) Big Cheese Photo(RF)/Picturequest; (b) Getty Images; I12 (bc) David R. Frazier/ The Image Works; (bc) David R. Frazier Photolibrary/Alamy

UNIT 1: 1A (c) Creasource/Corbis; 1 (t) Creasource/Corbis; 2 (br) Sean Cayton/ The Image Works; (br) Blend Images/Alamy; 3 (tl) Purestock / Alamy; (bl) Michael Newman/PhotoEdit; 11 (br) Getty Images; (bl) Robert Brenner/PhotoEdit; 12 (t) Cindy Charles/PhotoEdit; 13 (c) Tony Freeman/PhotoEdit; 17 (b) Walter Bibikow/ DanitaDelimont.com; (t) Corbis; 18 (l) Getty Images; 23 (bg) Tony Freeman/PhotoEdit; 24 (b) Ilene MacDonald/age fotostock; 25 (cr) Ocean/Corbis; (tr) Brand X Pictures/Getty Images; (cr) Syracuse Newspapers/The Images Works; 29 (b) Richard T. Nowitz/Corbis; (tr) Michael Heller/911 pictures; 30 (b) Construction Photography/Corbis; (tr) Jeffrey Greenberg/Photo Researchers, Inc.; (b) Gibson Stock Photo; 31 (tr) Digital Vision Ltd./Superstock ; 33 (c) Kayte M. Deioma/PhotoEdit; 35 (br) Jeff Greenberg/PhotoEdit; 36 (b) David Young-Wolff/PhotoEdit; (tr) Steve Skjold/Alamy; 37 (cr) Getty Images; 38 (br) Chris Cole/Getty Images; 40 (br) AP/WideWorld Photo; 41 (t) Time Life Pictures/Getty Images

UNIT 2: 49A (c) Jumper/Getty 49 (c)Jumper/Getty; (bcr) Colin Anderson/Corbis; 51 (bl) VEER; (cr) Getty Images; (tr) Felicia Martinez/PhotoEdit; 52 (br) Richard T. Nowitz / Corbis; 57 (tl) John E. Gilmore, III; (bl) www.distelphoto.com; 62 (bl) Galen Rowell/Peter Arnold. Inc.; (cr) Lester Lefkowitz/Corbis; 63 (bg) James Forte/Getty; (l) Ed Cooper Photo; (r) Getty Images; 64 (r) SuperStock, Inc./SuperStock; (cl) Vasapolli, Salvatore/Animals Animals; (cl) James Randklev/Getty; 65 (bg) Guy Jarvis; 66 (cr) Pat & Chuck Blackley; 67 (tr) Adam Jones/DanitaDelimont.com; (cl) Dennis Flaherty/PhotoResearchers, Inc.; (bl) Dennis MacDonald/Photri Images; (bg) Zach Holmes/Alamy; 68 (c) kord.com/age fotostock; 69 (c) Randall Hyman; (b) Dave Bartruff/Photolibrary; 70 (tl) Chuck Place; (cr) Joseph Sohm; Visions of America/Corbis; (cl) T. Hallstein/Outsight; (tr) Mark Richards/PhotoEdit; (c) Walter Bibikow/Getty Images; (br) The Granger Collection, New York; 71 (cr) Corbis; (cl) Najlah Feanny / Corbis; (c) Getty Images; 74 (b) altrendo images/Getty Images; 75 (cl) dkimages; (cr) Oscar Burriel/Photo Researchers, Inc. (bc) David Prince/Getty; (tr) Johnathon Kantor/Getty Images; (b) joSon/Getty Images; (tl) Nino Mascardi/The Image Bank/Getty Images; (c) Tom Brakefield/SuperStock; 76 (bl) istockphoto; (b) Kim Karpeles; (tr) 2002 The Taunton Press, Fine Woodworking Magazine; 77 (b) Jeff Greenberg/Index Stock Imagery/Photolibrary; (r) Dynamic Graphics Group/Creatas/Alamy; 78 (c) Marc Romanelli/Alamy; (bl) Johann Schumacher; 79 (t) David Frazier/Corbis; 82 (br) Montage/Getty Images; 83 (tl) Bettmann/Corbis; (tr) AP/WideWorld Photo; 84 (b) ThinkStock LLC/Getty Images; 85 (bg) AP Photo/Jean-Marc Bouju; (tl) Corbis ; (bl) Rainbow; (br) Tom Stewart/Corbis; 87 (tr) LWA/Corbis; 88 (c) Getty Images; (r) Kevin Dodge/Masterfile; 89 (tl) Alamy Images; (tc) Getty Images; (tr) Photodisc Green/Getty Images; (bl) Massachusetts Historical Society, Boston, MA, USA/Bridgeman Art Library

UNIT 3: 97A (cl) Gary Conner/Index Stock Imagery/Photolibrary; 97 (t) Gary Conner/Index Stock Imagery/Photolibrary; 98 (t) Photodisc/Getty Images; (br) David Young-Wolff/PhotoEdit; 99 (bl) NASA; (tl) Dennis MacDonald/PhotoEdit; (cr) Corbis; 100 (br) Tom and Pat Leeson; 104 (b) Bert Lane/Plimoth Plantation; 105 (c) Nik Wheeler/Corbis; 105 (fg) HMH; (tr) Photograph courtesy of Plimoth Plantation, Inc. www.plimoth.org; 107 Dennis Degnan / Corbis; 108 (b) The Granger Collection, New York; (t) Gary Ombler/Getty; 109 (tr) Stock Montage / Getty Images; 110 (b) Francis G. Mayer/Corbis; 111 (c) Corbis; (tr)

Corbis; (tl) The Granger Collection, New York; 112 (tr) The Granger Collection, New York; (br) Herbert Orth/Time & Life Pictures/Getty Images; 113 (b) North Wind Picture Archives/North Wind Productions; (t) Archiving Early America; 114 (tr) Lester Lefkowitz/Corbis; (bl) The Granger Collection, New York; 115 (r) Joseph Sohm; ChromoSohm/Corbis; (l) The Granger Collection, New York; 119 (tr) The Granger Collection; 120 (bc) Leif Skoogfors/Corbis; (cr) Alamy Images; 121 (tr) Tom and Pat Leeson; 122 (l) Alan Schein Photography/Corbis; (tr) Guy Crittenden/Index Stock Imagery/Photolibrary; (br) Getty Images/PhotoDisc; 123 (t) Joseph Sohm/Visions of America/Corbis; 124 (r) Alamy Images; 126 (r) John McGrail / PhiladelphiaImages.com; 127 (cl) Steve Hamblin/Alamy; (b) Michael Ventura; (tr) William Thomas Cain/Getty Images; (cr) Tim Shaffer/Reuters; 129 (b) Yogi/Corbis; (tr) Dennis MacDonald/PhotoEdit; (cl) Eric A. Clement/U.S. Navy/Getty Images; (cr) Chris Sorensen; 130 (bl) Philadelphia Museum of Art/Corbis; (br) PhotoLink/Photodisc/Getty Images; 131 (br) Getty Images; (cl) Library of Congress, Prints and Photographs Division [LC- USZ62-15195]; 132 (b) Michael Ventura; (tr) Tony Freeman/PhotoEdit; 133 (tr) Masterfile; 136 (bl) Ozaukee County Historical Society; (cl) Heinz-Dieter Falkenstein/Photolibrary; 137 (b) The Meridian StarAssociated Press

UNIT 4: 145A (t) SCPhotos/Alamy; 145 (t) SCPhotos/Alamy; 146 (tc) DeWitt Historical Society/Morton Collection/Getty Images; (br) Ariel Skelley/Corbis; 147 (cr) Ron Kimball/Ron Kimball Stock; (cr) Photolibrary; (r) DLILLC/Corbis; (tl) S.A. Kraulis/Masterfile; (bl) Paul Barton/Corbis; (tr) Getty Images Royalty Free; 148 (br) R. H. Charlton/Corbis; 158 (cr) Corbis; 159 (inset) Retrofile.com; 160 (l) Getty Images; (r) H. Armstrong Roberts/Classicstock; 161 (l) Getty Images; (r) Image from the Lower Cape Fear Historical Society Archives, Wilmington NC; 162 (l) H. Armstrong Roberts/ClassicStock; (r) George Marks/Retrofile/Getty Images; 164 (bl) H. Armstrong Roberts/Retrofile/Getty Images (b) Photolibrary; 166 (bl) Ewing Galloway/Photolibrary; (cr) Ewing Galloway/Photolibrary; (bc) Dave L. Ryan/Photolibrary; (br) Getty Images; 167 (bl) C Squared Studios/Photodisc Green/Getty Images; (tr) Dave L. Ryan/Photolibrary; (br) Schenectady Museum; Hall of Electrical History Foundation/Corbis; (tl) Schenectady Museum; Hall of Electrical History Foundation/Corbis; 168 (br) Hot Ideas/Index Stock Imagery/Photolibrary; (tr) Superstock RF; (cl) Hot Ideas/Index Stock Imagery/Photolibrary; 169 (tr) Getty Images; (c) Royalty-free/Corbis; (tl) Hot Ideas/Index Stock Imagery/Photolibrary; 170 (bc) Culver Pictures; 171 (cl) Lawrence Migdale; (tr) Will Hart/PhotoEdit; (br) Amy Etra/PhotoEdit; 174 (c) Hulton-Deutsch Collection/Corbis; (tr) Library of Congress, Prints and Photographs Division [LC-USZ62-95793]; (b) Sarah Fabian-Baddiel/Photolibrary; 175 (tr) Brown Brothers; (cr) Dana White/PhotoEdit; 177 (cl) Gloria Rejune Adams/Old School Square; (tcl) Blackwell History of Education Museum; (bl) Blackwell History of Education Museum; (tl) The Granger Collection, New York; (tr) Getty Images; (br) Getty Images/Photodisc; 178 (br) Jim Whitmer Photography; (cr) Indiana Historical Society; (cr) Getty ; 179 (c) Photo Agora; (c) Scott Olsen/

Getty; 180 (cr) National Museum of American History, Smithsonian Institution; 181 (cr) www.distelphoto.com; (tr) Jacky Naegelen/X00198/Reuters/Corbis; 182 (br) Amy Etra/PhotoEdit; (bc) Getty Images/Photodisc; 184 (b) Garry DeLong/Alamy; (bl) Ralph E. Gray/National Geographic Society/Corbis; 185 (c) Brian A. Vikander/Corbis; 186 (r) Museum of Flight/Corbis; (tc) Hulton/Archive/Getty Images;(c) Culver Pictures; (b) Brown Brothers; 187 (tr) Felix Clouzot/Getty Images; (tl) Robert Maust/Photo Agora; (c) Thomas Mayer/Peter Arnold, Inc.; (b) John McGrail Photography; 189 (tl) Getty Images; 192 (br) NASA; 193 (t) NASA

UNIT 5: 201A (bl) Bob Thomas/Getty Images; (tr) Raymond Gehman/Corbis; (tl) Superstock; [blind 201B] (tl) Patrick Olear/PhotoEdit; (cr) Raymond Gehman/Corbis; 201 (tr) Zephyr Picture/Index Stock/Photolibrary; (cl) Bob Thomas/Getty Images; (cr) Superstock; 202 (br) Popperfoto / Alamy; 203 (bl) Laura Dwight / Photo Edit; (cr) Brand X / Robertstock.com; (tl) Bettmann/Corbis; (tr) Corbis; 204 (br) StockByte/Getty Images; 212 (bl) Lawrence Migdale / Pix; 213 (br) City of Hackensack; 214 (cr) John Bigelow Taylor / Art Resource, NY; (br) Jerry Jacka Photography; (bl) Boltin Picture Library/Bridgeman Art Library; (tl) Werner Forman / Art Resource, NY; (c) Brooklyn Museum/Corbis; 215 (tr) Phil Schermeister/Corbis; 218 (br) John Elk, III; 219 (tl) The Granger Collection, New York; 222 (cl) Bill Aron/PhotoEdit; (cr) Gary Conner/PhotoEdit; (bc) David Young-Wolff/PhotoEdit; 223 (cr) Paul Hellander/Danita Delimont Stock Photography; (cl) Ariel Skelley/Corbis; 224 (c) Library of Congress Prints & Photographs Division; 226 (c) BananaStock/Jupiterimages; (r) PictureQuest; 227 (b) AP/Wide World Photos; (tl) PhotoDisc/Jupiterimages; (tc) Alamy Images; (tr) Alamy Images; 231 (tl) Bob Krist/Corbis; (tr) Richard A. Cooke/Corbis; 233 (bg) A. Ramey/PhotoEdit; 234 (bg) Jonathan Nourok/PhotoEdit; 235 (tl) Robert Brenner/PhotoEdit; 239 (tl) Friedrich Stark / Peter Arnold, Inc.; (tr) Sudhakar Chandra 2005; 240 (cr) Frans Lemmens / Peter Arnold, Inc.; (cl) Danita Delimont/Getty

UNIT 6: 249A (c) Damir Frkovic/Masterfile; 249 (t) Damir Frkovic/Masterfile; 250 (tc) AP/WideWorld Photo; (br) Danita Delimont/Alamy; 251 (cr) Mary Kate Denny / Photo Edit; (bl) Bob Donaldson/Pittsburg Post-Gazette; (tr) Harcourt; 252 (br) Getty Images/PhotoDisc; 260 (bc) Ron Kimball; (cl) David Young-Wolff/PhotoEdit; (cr) Ed Young/Corbis; 261 (tc) Roger Ball Photography; (tl) David Young-Wolff/PhotoEdit; (tr) Michael Newman/PhotoEdit; 262 (bl) Harcourt; (tr) Jeff Dunn/Photolibrary; 263 (tl) Getty Images; (tr) Jonathan Nourok/PhotoEdit; 266 (tc) Getty Images/Photodisc; (tr) Alamy Images; 267 (bl) The Granger Collection, New York; (tl) Getty Images; (tc) Getty Images; (tr) Alamy Images; 270 (c) Photophile; 271 (bg) John Zoiner; (br) Lewis Wickes Hine/Corbis; 272 (l) Anne Flinn Powell/Index Stock/Photolibrary; 275 (r) Pierre Arsenault / Masterfile; 276 (br) Arthur Schatz/Time & Life Pictures/Getty Images; 277 (cr) Michael Salas/Time Life Pictures/Getty Images; (tc) AP/Wide World Photos; (tl) Arthur Schatz/Time Life Pictures/Getty Images; 280 (r) Lawrence Migdale; 281 (l) Jeff Greenberg/PhotoEdit; 284 (b) David Young-Wolff/PhotoEdit; 287 (cl) Getty Images;

(tr) Photodisc/Getty Images; 288 (cr) Brendan Wehrung; 289 (bg) Corbis; (tl) Brendan Wehrung; (tr) Brendan Wehrung; (bl) Brendan Wehrung; (cr) Brendan Wehrung; 290 (bc) Gale Zucker Photography; 291 (bg) John Zoiner; (t) Getty Images; (bl) Gale Zucker Photography; (br) Getty Images; 292 (tl) Gale Zucker Photography; (br) Gale Zucker Photography; 293 (br) Gale Zucker Photography; (tl) Gale Zucker Photography; 294 (tr) Gale Zucker Photography; 294 (bl) Gale Zucker Photography

ENDMATTER: R10 (c) C Squared Studios/Photodisc/Getty Images; BACK COVER: (tl) Bob Rowan; Progressive Image/Corbis

All other photos © Houghton Mifflin Harcourt School Publishers.

Typeset in *HSP The Sans* and/or *HSS The Sans*, modified for primary legibility from the font *The Sans*, from LucasFonts.